reNEWed
how Jesus transforms your mind

SHANE CALLICUTT

Copyright © 2017 by Shane Callicutt

All rights reserved. No part of this publication may be reproduced, distributed, or transmitted in any form or by any means, including photocopying, recording, or other electronic or mechanical methods, without the prior written permission of the publisher, except in the case of brief quotations embodied in critical reviews and certain other noncommercial uses permitted by copyright law. For permission requests, contact the author via the website listed below.

Shane Callicutt
www.shaneshack.com

Unless otherwise noted, all Scripture quotations are from the ESV® Bible (The Holy Bible, English Standard Version®), copyright © 2001 by Crossway, a publishing ministry of Good News Publishers. Used by permission. All rights reserved. Any **bold** or *italicized* words within Scripture quotations have been added by the author for emphasis.

Thank you to Matt and Cathy for reviewing this in your spare time. Thanks again to Sharon for your editing skills. You all have blessed me and given me insight. I appreciate it immensely.

My praise and love to Radene for being my faithful bride and reading everything I hand her. Her love is a constant blessing to me, and she is by far my most favorite person on the planet.

This book is for my daughters, Phoebe and Ayva. I love you ferociously. Do yourselves a favor and learn these things faster than I did.

THE CONTENTS

Introduction — 1

(CHAPTER ONE)
New Heart, Old Mind — 9

(CHAPTER TWO)
Where It All Begins — 33

(CHAPTER THREE)
Out With The Old — 55

(CHAPTER FOUR)
In With The New — 75

(CHAPTER FIVE)
Keeping a Clean House — 99

(CHAPTER SIX)
Spiritual Stamina — 123

(CHAPTER SEVEN)
The Mind of Christ — 145

In Closing — 167

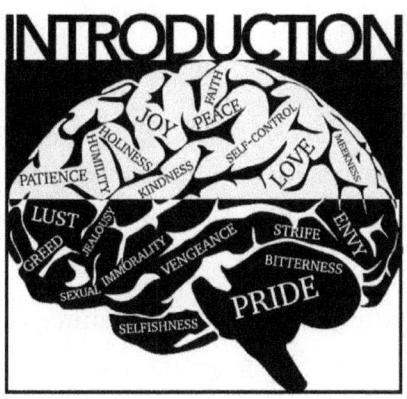

INTRODUCTION

Of late in my life, I have been thinking a lot about what it means to thrive. I've only barely dipped my feet into my forties, and if anything has been crystal clear to me, it's this: I want my forties to be the most productive decade of my life yet. That means a lot of things for me personally. Historically I'm not an especially organized person, although I do get things done most of the time. For me to be more productive, that will have to change. I will need to sharpen my skills, learn new ones, increase my discipline, and up my game organizationally speaking. Sadly, this is just dealing with my talents and skills, not even touching things spiritually.

Spiritual flourishing is something that needs discussion. What does it mean to thrive spiritually? If you asked ten different Christians, you might get ten different answers. That's unfortunate because the Bible isn't vague on this topic. The problem I've noticed is churches are the ones that make this complicated. Hear me, I love the church, but denominationalism, individualism, and the desire to make Jesus into our own personalized savior has produced a variety of methodologies, catechisms, statements of faith, and formulaic approaches for spiritual flourishing.

In my own personal church experience from Baptist churches, the focus was very firmly upon avoiding sin, prayer, and reading the Bible, but not much else. The church (in general) is great at teaching us how to modify our behavior but not at killing the source of the behavior. *Don't smoke. Don't chew. Don't date those who do.* And, more recently, *don't even date.* We chop away at the behavioral weeds as they crop up, modifying the behavior of our life, but not really getting at the roots. Eventually you will get fatigued from cutting down the same things over and over. And when you're fatigued, you're vulnerable to temptation. No garden can thrive unless the weeds are removed at the root, and no spiritual life can flourish unless the roots of our sins are exposed and uprooted.

I was churched enough as a teenager and young adult to have heard Jeremiah 17:9 over and over: *The heart is deceitful above all things, and desperately sick; who can understand it?* I had been taught that the human heart is wicked and nothing good can come from it. That was kind of depressing. The thought that even as a Christian, our hearts are still filled with evil and wickedness kind of leaves you feeling a little helpless. But then one day I heard a pastor on the radio teaching about a new heart, something that was never explained to me. When

God saves us he gives us a new heart, a new spirit, and he gives us his Spirit. This was foretold by the prophet Ezekiel.

> And I will give you a new heart, and a new spirit I will put within you. And I will remove the heart of stone from your flesh and give you a heart of flesh. And I will put my Spirit within you, and cause you to walk in my statutes and be careful to obey my rules. (Ezekiel 36:26-27)

This was a game changer! The understanding that as a believer I now have a new heart and new spirit slowly shifted my focus. My new desires were to love God and live a life that pleases him, but where everything was getting messed up was *my mind*. I had new desires, but I had an old mind. And for all believers, this is where the epicenter of our conflict erupts. The godly new desires of your new heart run head-on with your old thinking. And herein is the focus of Renewed. How does Jesus transform your mind?

> Do not be conformed to this world, but be transformed by the *renewal of your mind*, that by testing you may discern what is the will of God, what is good and acceptable and perfect. (Romans 12:2)

This is the banner verse for this book. In it we find both the action and the reason. The way we thrive spiritually is by renewing our minds. The reason renewing our minds is so important is because it sharpens our ability to discern the will of God for our lives. Sounds simple enough, but as you engage in mind renewal, you will find that it is in fact *the* battle of the Christian life. Everything we do, every way we react is all connected to how we think. The fight for mind renewal is the most important fight of the Christian life because from its spoils you will either flourish or languish.

In this introduction, let me offer a few definitions and some concepts that will serve us throughout the rest of this volume. In doing this here, I won't have to re-explain them every time they come up. First a few definitions in layman's terms.

- **Old self**: this is the man or woman you were before your new birth into the kingdom of God. This person died the day you were born again, yet it still remains with you and it still has an appetite.
- **New self**: this is the new man or woman that was born the moment the Holy Spirit birthed you into the kingdom of God. This person has a new heart, new godly desires, and wants to please God above all else.
- **The heart**: this is the source of all emotions and desires in a person's life. Whatever is in the heart sets the course of a person's life.
- **The mind**: this is the place in all of us where the desires of our hearts are processed. Plans are formed and put into action in the mind. It's also the place

where we decide what to do with the physical and emotional needs of our lives.

- **Stronghold:** this is a fortress of thoughts.[1] Your view of the world, how you handle struggle and victory, how you view yourself are all systems of thoughts that come together to form a stronghold which dictates how you process life. Strongholds can be good *and* they can be destructive *(this isn't my definition, but it's probably the best and simplest one I've heard).*

For sure, these definitions are not complete, but I believe they communicate the weight and intention necessary to carry on our conversation. At times, I may delve a little deeper into these definitions, but what is said here will set the baseline from which you can know what I mean. Now, here's a few concepts that I want to define up front for the same purpose of creating a baseline of understanding.

Sanctification is a word that means the process of Christian growth and maturity. To sanctify something means to set it apart for a special purpose. Sanctification happens to all believers because God has promised to complete the work of redemption that he began in us when he saved us. Philippians 1:6 says, *". . . he who began a good work in you will bring it to completion at the day of Jesus Christ."* Inherent in this promise is a process that God *will* put us through to hone our character and sharpen our discernment so that we *will* live like Jesus in what remains of our lives on this earth. Our sanctification will happen, and you could say that our pace through sanctification depends upon our willingness to bend to the process. One thing that I've found, and you can see it in the lives of many saints in the Scripture, is that God will keep trying to teach you the same lesson again and again until you get it. And many times with each attempt to teach comes a greater severity! These days I'm trying hard to *get it* the first time!

Spiritual warfare is another Christian phrase that gets a lot of mileage but has a varied understanding throughout the Church. I'm not about to tear down anyone's definitions, but again I simply want to establish a basic understanding. Spiritual warfare has two basic forms. First, it is the fight in which each Christian engages to kill their old desires in favor of the new ones received with the new heart. This is internal and has to do with motives and strongholds. Second, it's the fight in which we engage through prayer on behalf of other people. When I pray for someone, I am engaging in a spiritual battle on their behalf. This is also called *intercessory prayer* because we are interceding with God on someone's behalf.

This book is going to walk through the muddy waters of how these concepts are a daily part of the transformation of your mind. I say muddy waters because I'm not the first person to attempt to write on this issue. Others have traversed these waters before me, and more will after me. What I hope to do is bring some clarity to this issue which, in my experience, has suffered from either being underdeveloped or overcomplicated. Jesus wants us to live differently than we once did. He wants to lead us in renewing our way of thinking because the mind is where it all gets feet and begins coming to life. Once a feeling or an idea gets traction in your life, it eventually produces action. Change the way you think and your actions will follow. Jesus knows this: renew your mind, recreate your life.

References:
1. I'm giving credit to either Dr. Eric Mason or Evangelist Ken Freeman for this definition. I'm positive I heard one of them say it, I'm just coming up short on remembering which one.

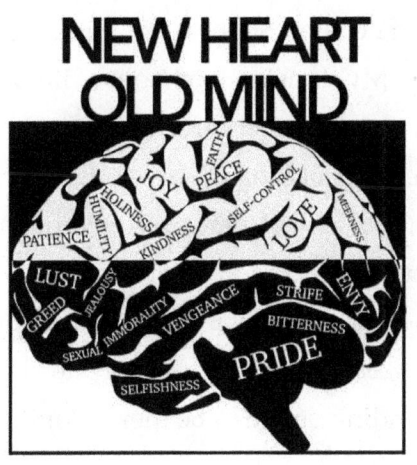

"War is hell." General William Tecumseh Sherman is credited with coining this phrase, although my initial attempts to search out when and where he uttered those words fell flat. The best I could find in an Internet search was a Wikipedia article where it only says he *may* have uttered those words in an address to the Michigan Military Academy on Jun 19, 1879 [1]. Whether or not he actually said *war is hell*, is not the point. However, he did say in a letter to the mayor of Atlanta that "war is cruelty."[2] In this letter, he explained the necessity of evacuating Atlanta before his Union troops burned the city on November 12, 1864.

I've never been to war. As a senior in high school in 1994, I was almost convinced to join the Navy, but upon speaking with a recruiter on the phone, my heart changed and I abandoned those plans. Had I joined, I might have seen deployment to hot spots across the globe, but in the mid to late nineties, the United States wasn't involved in any large-scale conflicts. My decision to choose a different path didn't lessen my love and respect for the military one bit. In fact, although I never spoke of it out loud, after the attacks of September 11, 2001, I had some fleeting thoughts of enlisting. I was 25, young, able-bodied, and angry. But my wife, Radene, was two months pregnant with our first child, Phoebe. My greater ministry, my greater love, was living with me, depending on me to be there. And I had no further thoughts about it.

I've always been relationally close to people who have served in the military. My father served in the Air Force in the early 1950s. My Uncle Kenny served in the Army around the same time. I have a cousin, Steve, who served in the Air Force and retired as a Colonel. Today I have several friends who are serving or have served in the Marines and Navy. I recently attended a good friend's retirement ceremony from the Marines, and my heart was once again stirred considering how my life would've been different had I enlisted.

I suppose many of us have similar stories. Many of us know someone who has served, or is currently serving, in the military. To serve in the military has been an honorable tradition in this nation. Though you can argue that not everyone in the military is honorable, the tradition of service and the training that is received equips the soldier to be an honorable person. It's the hearts of men that choose whether or not to use what has been given to them for the good of others or for selfish ambition.

The heart is a big deal. The heart is what sets the course of our lives. Jesus made it very clear that whatever is in the heart manifests itself outwardly.

> The good person out of the good treasure of his heart produces good, and the evil person out of his evil treasure produces evil, for out of the abundance of the heart his mouth speaks. (Luke 6:45)

In other words, you can know a great deal about what's in a person's heart by their words. We don't really need anyone to snitch on us; eventually we give ourselves away because whatever is in our hearts leaks out into our words and actions.

It's a popular thing in our culture to instruct people to follow their hearts. We've all known someone, or been the person who is seeking answers to life's questions. When we arrive at an intersection of life, we often stand there wondering which way to turn. It's a lot like Tom Hank's character, Chuck Nolen, at the end of the movie *Castaway*. He sits at the intersection of two dirt roads on the Texas plains trying to decide which way he should go. One way is uncertain, the other way leads to an attractive woman to whom he just delivered the only FedEx package that he didn't open while he was stranded on his island.

The movie ends before we know what he chose, but it's implied that he went back for the woman. We would say that he followed his heart. Jesus would say that he's been following his heart all along. We always pursue the things we treasure. According to Luke 6:45, what we produce – the fruit of our lives – is the product of our pursuit for what we find most valuable. Jesus says elsewhere:

> For where your treasure is, there your heart will be also. (Matthew 6:21)

Our hearts will always be in pursuit of what we treasure most. There is no other way. We're created to pursue pleasure, beauty, treasure, value, and worth. And whatever we believe will increase those things in our lives, that is what we will pursue. Therefore, whatever you find in your heart, it's there because you value it most.

What about things like hatred and anger? Why would anyone value those qualities? We value them so long as they serve us in reaching our treasure. If you value revenge, if you value payback, if you hold a grudge from having been wronged, then what most people consider negative emotions will be valued because they serve you in your quest for vengeance.

If being popular is your treasure, then whatever serves you in achieving that goal will fill your heart. If being successful is your treasure, then your heart will be filled with whatever it takes to become successful. If you objectify and lust over the opposite sex, then your heart will be filled with adultery and envy. And so forth and so on; the things that fill your heart are all in the service of helping you achieve your greatest treasure.

The human heart was designed to work this way. It's not an accident. Our hearts don't work this way because we're ruined by the Fall. God designed the human heart to pursue its desires with pit bull tenacity. Which is simultaneously our greatest problem and our greatest asset. Jesus said that the good person, out of the good treasure of his heart produces good. So if we have good treasure in our hearts, then the fruit of our lives will be good fruit. But it works both ways. If our treasure is wicked, then our fruit will be wicked. Follow me closely because I'm about to connect a few Scripture dots.

Dot one: Jesus said it is the good person who has good treasure, and therefore good fruit. Jesus also said *no one is good, except God alone* (Luke 18:19). So God is the only good guy in the universe (and by implication Jesus, because he's the God-the-Son person of the God-head). That leaves all of us squarely in the evil camp. So here's the deal: all of our hearts are helplessly wicked. Therefore, none of us, on our own, can produce good fruit.

Dot two: we are born spiritually dead and disconnected from God (Ephesians 2:1). So even though your heart was designed to pursue its desires tenaciously, because we're born spiritually dead, we desperately seek our happiness in created things instead of our Creator. Our hearts make *lower case gods* out of earthly things that inevitably crumble under the weight of our expectations. This is why the prophet Jeremiah says, *"The heart is deceitful above all things, and desperately sick; who can understand it?"* (17:9) It is deceitful because it leads you to false gods, and it's beyond understanding because it never ceases to disappoint us by leading us from god to god to god, always promising the next one will be better but never delivering on that promise.

Dot three: the only solution for us has to be a rebirth. Jesus famously said to Nicodemus, *"Truly, truly, I say to you, unless one is born again he cannot see the kingdom of God."* (John 3:3) In other words, because we're born spiritually dead and disconnected from God, the only solution for us to enter God's kingdom is a spiritual rebirth because as one might learn from reading the Sermon on the Mount, the bar for entering God's kingdom is impossible for the natural born man to achieve.

Dot four: three things happen in the new birth. The prophet Ezekiel lines them out for us. *"I will give you a **new heart** . . . a **new spirit** I will put within you . . . I will put **my Spirit** within you."* (Ezekiel 36:26-27) The new heart and new spirit together form what the Apostle Paul calls the *new self* (Ephesians 4:24, Colossians 3:10). This new self is the new creation spoken of in 2 Corinthians 5:17:

> Therefore, if anyone is in Christ, he is a *new creation*. The old has passed away; behold, the new has come. (emphasis added)

But not only do we experience the birth of our new self, God also plants the Holy Spirit with in us to *"cause you to walk in my statutes and be careful to obey my rules."* (Ezekiel 36:27) This doesn't mean that he takes over and turns us into robots, forcing us into obedience. The Holy Spirit causes us to obey through persuasion, not coercion. He shows us the beauty of Christ, reminds us of his love and sacrifice, and offers us a choice to love and honor Christ's commands in light of the cross or pursue our own selfish desires. The new self is full of desires to heed the Holy Spirit's leading. And this is where the fight begins.

I remember rather vividly the worst spanking I ever received. It was first grade and we had a babysitter named Tracy. As I recall she was a nice woman, but she was strict. My sisters and I would get off the school bus at her home every afternoon and remain there until my parents got off work. As soon as we walked in the door, the first order of business was to do our homework. No questions, no exceptions, no fun could be had until the homework was complete.

If you read Recreated, you'll recall that I was a fairly compliant child. I usually obeyed and did what was asked of me, even if grumbling the whole way. But for some reason, one afternoon on the bus ride home I got a wild idea. I was tired of being forced to do my homework as soon as we walked in the door. I reasoned to myself that if, instead of walking directly inside her house, I would go around back and find a place to play before she could make me do homework I would beat the system; have some fun first, and do homework later. To my first grade brain, that was a perfect plan. She never stood outside waiting for us, so she would never see me bolt around back. Perfect!

As soon as my feet hit the ground from the bus, I made a b-line for her back yard. This all might've been perfect had I not chosen such a well-hidden place to play. Tracy had a German Shepherd, which I loved dearly. He was underneath her deck resting. I saw him and proceeded to crawl under the deck to play with him. I pet him, played fetch with a stick that was under the deck, and had a really fun time.

My plan was to play for only a short time, then go inside and do my homework. By the time I decided it was time to go in, almost an hour and a half had passed. Of course I didn't realize this, that is until I walked in her back door to see Tracy in a panic. She had *no idea* where I had been. She had called my mom, so she was on her way home early to presumably start a search party. But it still hadn't registered in my mind what the big fuss was. I was right outside the whole time, perfectly safe, perfectly content. Why was Tracy so upset with me?

Slowly the reality began to settle in. It was almost perfect. My understanding aligned with the reality of the situation the moment my mom's car pulled into Tracy's driveway. I was in *huge* trouble. In fact, my mom, who was a strict disciplinarian, was so angry with me that she wouldn't touch me. She uttered those words that every child shudders to hear: *wait until your dad gets home!*

When we got home, all I could do was curl up like an infant in my room and wait. It seemed like hours, but in reality it was probably only thirty minutes before my dad arrived home from work. I don't recall any yelling. Just silence. Then in dramatic fashion, my bedroom door opened and my dad stood there with his chosen instrument of punishment: a short leather strap which he called the *razor strap*. A horrible name for a tool of discipline, but in reality it was a short piece of leather from a belt of some sort that had worn out long ago. Regardless, this razor strap struck fear into the hearts of me and my sisters. I retreated into the corner as far as I could, but no corner of my bedroom was far enough away to escape the reach of the razor strap. And there was much wailing and gnashing of teeth.

To me, this is a great picture of the kind of decisions we have to make all the time. I knew what I was supposed to do, but I thought I had a better plan. My plan was going to accomplish both fun and homework, but it went south quickly because I underestimated my strengths and weaknesses. My desire to play was far stronger, far more dominating than my desire to do my homework. Not only that, I underestimated the ramifications of not being where I was supposed to be. My plan had unintended consequences and Tracy was wounded because of my plan. (Consequently, we had a new baby sitter within days.) My plan affected

Tracy, it affected my parents, and it affected the comfort of my hind parts.

The new self knows. The new self has a heart that is filled with desires to please God. The new self has the Holy Spirit offering instruction and recall of the Word as we navigate the path before us. Because of the new self and the Holy Spirit, every believer is fully equipped to listen to and obey God's leading.

> His divine power has granted to us all things that pertain to life and godliness, through the knowledge of him who called us to his own glory and excellence, (2 Peter 1:3)

But the reason we don't always obey the Holy Spirit is because there's something still within us that tells us there's a better way. Nearly every believer has experienced the Spirit of God saying *do this* and then another voice says *yeah, but*. That other voice is the voice of a dead man. Yes, it's true. You hear dead people . . . at least one. Let me explain.

The new birth is also a death. The day your new self is born, the old self dies. That's why 2 Corinthians 5:17 says *the old has passed away*. Take that a step further, Paul reminds us in Romans chapter six that:

> We know that our old self was crucified with him in order that the body of sin might be brought to nothing,

so that we would no longer be enslaved to sin. (Romans 6:6)

The moment the new self is born, the old self is crucified with Christ. Yet, there's this pesky problem that although dead, the old self still has a voice, still has an appetite, and still tries to enforce its will. In Recreated I likened the old self to a zombie, and I still think the comparison is appropriate. The myth of zombies is that they are dead people whose decomposed bodies have risen to roam the earth and eat the living. The old self is similar. He's dead, but he still has an appetite. He's dead but he still consumes as much of your life has he can.

What gives the old self this kind of staying power? If he's dead, why is he still hanging on? Put simply, the new birth gives us a new self, complete with new heart and new spirit, but we still have a *fallen body* and a *fallen mind*. The Bible calls our fallen body and mind, *the flesh*. The flesh is the corrupted, unredeemed part of our lives that remains with us until it dies. For believers it is the remaining vestige of the curse that came upon humanity when Adam and Eve sinned. It remains with us until it suffers its final physical death. The flesh is what gives the old self it's staying power. In a manner of speaking, the flesh is life support for the old man. The old man is clinically dead, but the flesh is the machinery that's keeps giving it a pulse. Let me flesh out *the flesh*.

The first part of the flesh is our physical bodies. In its original design, before Adam and Eve sinned, it had needs and desires that were completely fulfilled through what God had provided in the Garden of Eden. God provided food for hunger. God provided water for thirst. God gave Adam and Eve each other in marriage for sexual desire and building a family. Everything that the body desired, God had provided it. And our bodies were satisfied completely with God's provisions. In fact, they were so perfectly satisfied and sustained by God, they were physically perfect and immortal.

But when Adam and Eve sinned, the consequences of their choice brought a curse upon the physical body. First of all, it would eventually die. There were other things as well, but for our purposes here I'm zooming in on the physical death aspect. These bodies, that were once immortal, were now destined to die because sin brings death. Adam and Eve's choice to sin by violating the *only* law that God gave them brought death into the human condition. And from that moment their perfect, immortal bodies were corrupted and began experiencing a slow decay.

The second part of the flesh is our mind. The mind is an interesting thing. Did you know that your brain has been designed for efficiency? When God designed the human brain, he wired it so that it would accomplish a maximum of work with a minimum of effort. It is estimated that while we actually do use one hundred percent of our brain's capacity (contrary to the ten percent myth), only one to sixteen percent of our neurons are active at any given moment.[3] So we have this incredibly efficient brain that God has designed to accomplish its mission with minimal energy cost to the rest of the body. Because of its design your mind will always try to find the fastest, quickest, most efficient route to satisfaction.

Before the Fall, in the Garden of Eden, Adam and Eve had perfect satisfaction with our Creator. Their spirits and their bodies were uncorrupted by sin so there was nothing standing between them and their fellowship with God. They were completely sustained by their connection with God. But when they chose to sin, they died spiritually. And when that spiritual connection with God was severed, I believe they began to die physically. The spiritual connection sustained the immortality of the physical.

When Adam and Eve lost their spiritual connection with God, it was then up to them to find that divine satisfaction again. Their minds, having the efficient brains that God had designed for them, immediately began trying to restore the connection that brought the satisfaction to life that they experienced in the Garden. Since they were now dead spiritually, they (and consequently, we all) turned to created things, which are quicker and easier to bring a momentary satisfaction, but are unable to sustain us. So our minds move quickly and efficiently from source to source trying to bring a longer lasting satisfaction to life, desperately trying to fill the void left from our first ancestors' Fall. And because our minds are part of our fallen physical bodies, after we are born again we have to retrain our minds to go against their design and once again find a lasting satisfaction in God, which is hard, instead of created things, which is easy but temporary. All that to say this: even with the new self and the Holy Spirit inside, the mind is going to work against you because it is designed to take the path of least resistance.

So, this life support system for the old man, the flesh, the combined physical desires of our fallen physical bodies, and the efficiency of our fallen minds, is a formidable enemy. Whenever the body's desires are stirred, the mind will seek out the easiest path to satisfaction. But you know it's more complicated than this. It's not always the mind catering to the bodies desires. Sometimes its flip-flopped. Consider the phenomenon of emotional eating. The mind becomes stressed, and even though there is no physical hunger, the mind convinces us that food will bring a momentary satisfaction to dull the stress. So we eat. There is in fact a complex dynamic between the mind and the body that should always keep the new self on its toes. The flesh will always suggest that there is a better, faster, more satisfying way to fulfill your desires; even the good desires that come from your new self.

This is where ninety-five percent of the Christian battle happens. What is the solution? We have a new heart and an old mind. The new heart is always pointing us to God. The old mind is always suggesting enticing detours. God knows this and he has prescribed for us how to handle it in his Word. Satan knows this too, and he has baited the path with things that will entice the old mind. When Jesus told Peter, James and John that he was going to make them fishers of men, he was actually encroaching into the Devil's favorite pass time. Satan is also a fisher of men because beneath the bait is a sharp hook that will snag us and pull us places where we don't want to go.

Once upon a time, I really enjoyed fishing. Mostly as a kid. Today I can take it or leave it, but occasionally I enjoy going out on the water with friends. Not much has changed about fishing through the centuries. Sure, now we have technology that helps us locate the fish, but knowing where the fish are located makes no guarantee of catching any of them if you don't know how to lure. First you must know *what* the fish are hungry for. Any old food won't work. As much as I might like a Snickers bar, putting a hunk of Snickers on a hook won't catch a fish. Second, you need to know *when* the fish are most likely to bite. Any old time of the day isn't always the best time to catch a fish. You have to lure them when the conditions are ripe for their appetite.

If Satan has anything, he has multiple PhDs on humanity. He knows how to lure us. He knows what our appetites want and he has expert timing for when we are most likely to take the bait and get hooked. So he lays out a line of baits, conceals the hook, and waits. He doesn't really have to do much else. Once we're hooked, we're stuck and rendered ineffective. And just like fish, we often nibble at the bait for a bit, tasting it without biting, flirting with the idea of taking the whole thing in, but not all at once at first. Then after a few tastes, we bite, and the hook painfully penetrates our flesh and we find ourselves trapped because it would be more painful and more damaging to pull the hook out than it was to be pierced in the first place. Removing the hook from a fish often leaves a larger wound than the hook made on entry. The same is true for us.

The fallen mind sees the bait. It reasons that a taste won't hurt. But the new self knows this isn't what God wants. So the battle rages. If we allow the mind to prevail, once the first taste is taken, control of this goes from mind to body. Now the body wants more, and the mind is happy to oblige by finding ways to get another taste. And another. And another. Then a taste isn't enough. The bite is taken, the hook is lodged, and we are immobilized until we allow someone else to painfully remove the hook.

> Wretched man that I am! Who will deliver me from this ***body of death***? (Romans 7:24)

> ... among whom we all once lived in the passions of our flesh, ***carrying out the desires of the body and the mind***, and were by nature children of wrath, like the rest of mankind. (Ephesians 2:3)

What is the solution? Many Christians blame the heart. They lean on Jeremiah and say that our hearts are wicked and deceitful. But if I have a new heart and a new spirit, that cannot be true. Thankfully, the New Testament consistently tells us the solution. It never says renew your heart because it's already new (as a side note, neither does it ever say rededicate your life). It does, however, always say on repeat, *renew your mind*. Notice the emphasis in each of the following verses.

> For to set the mind on the flesh is death, **but to set the mind on the Spirit is life and peace.** (Romans 8:6)

> Do not be conformed to this world, **but be transformed by the renewal of your mind,** that by testing you may discern what is the will of God, what is good and acceptable and perfect. (Romans 12:2)

> Finally, brothers, whatever is true, whatever is honorable, whatever is just, whatever is pure, whatever is lovely, whatever is commendable, if there is any excellence, if there is anything worthy of praise, **think about these things.** (Philippians 4:8)

> Therefore, **preparing your minds for action, and being sober-minded,** set your hope fully on the grace that will be brought to you at the revelation of Jesus Christ. (1 Peter 1:13)

Could it be that many of us have fought this war with the flesh – some for a long time – with misguided tactics? Have we ceded ground in the war against sin by neglecting the discipline of mind renewal? Here's the deal. If we are born again, even with the Holy Spirit as our helper, the new self (new heart and new spirit) has no chance of growth and development if we do not engage in the discipline of mind renewal. If the mind is left *as is* it will never learn how to deal with things in a new way. It will always resort to the path of least resistance method of resolving problems. This is where so many Christians find themselves. Their new hearts want to honor the Lord and do right by Him, but their undisciplined minds have no categories for how to do it. It feels like a stalemate. I've been there. I've sat in my bedroom, frustrated with life, with all sorts of good desires to please God, but my mind kept leading me astray.

I think many Christians know exactly what I'm talking about. And when you find yourself at this stalemate, you're good for nothing because you're immobilized, unable to do anything. You want to follow Jesus, but your mind keeps pulling you in the other direction. You feel stretched thin from the tug-of-war between your new heart and your old mind. What's the answer? *Renew your mind!* We'll dive into this deeper later, but for now look closer at each of the verses I just listed.

Set your mind on the Spirit. What does that mean? To set your mind on the Spirit literally means give control of your thought life to the Holy Spirit. If you find your mind adrift, lost in thought, ask the Holy Spirit if these thoughts are pleasing to him. Some thoughts you *know* are contrary to the Spirit. Others aren't so clear. But the bottom line is that you should have an ongoing conversation with the Holy Spirit about your thought life. This requires that you begin relating directly and personally with the Holy Spirit as a person, not a force. The Holy Spirit has a personality, has feelings, similar to how you and I do. If he can be grieved (Ephesians 4:30), then it stands to reason that he can also be made happy. Perhaps the starting line for some of us is to simply recognize that the Holy Spirit is more than a force, but a person who desires conversation and fellowship. Then you can proceed to conversations about your thought life.

But be transformed by the renewal of your mind. The renewal of the mind is key to understanding the will of God. And *what is God's will for my life* may be in the top five of all questions that Christians ask. The truth about the question is that ninety percent of the answer is actually super simple. Romans 12:2 clearly tells us that God's will can only be understood by a renewed mind. That's because ninety percent of God's will for our lives is spelled out in his Word. So if you want to know the will of God, you must renew your mind by reading his Word. Putting the Word of God into your mind by reading it, meditating on it, and memorizing will renew the way your mind thinks. Then when situations arise that need decisions, ninety percent of the time, you'll know the answer. The other ten percent – like which job should I take, or which home should I buy – are found in knowing the active voice of the Holy Spirit in your life (see the previous paragraph).

Think about these things. The thought life is a key indicator of your spiritual temperature. When your mind wanders, where does it go? What is the general tone of your meandering thought life? It's easy to have focus when the job or task at hand demands focus. But what about when there are no immediate demands? What you think about when there's nothing demanding your thoughts is one indicator of where you are spiritually. The Word instructs us to direct our thoughts to whatever is true, honorable, just, pure, lovely, commendable, excellent, and praiseworthy. Unless you wrangle your entire thought life into obedience to this level of discipline, your mind will continue to work against the desires of your new heart.

Preparing your minds for action, and be sober-minded. Renewing the mind is also a preparation for action. No one knows what each moment may bring. If you've been pouring the Word into your mind, and disciplining your thought life to please the Holy Spirit, this makes you ready for whatever may come. It keeps things real. Contrary to what we see, the *real* world is the world unseen. It's easy to say that the battle in the unseen generally spills over into our world through sin, but one specific way is through undisciplined believers' fallen thinking. Paul declares our battle is not against flesh and blood, but against spiritual powers of darkness (Ephesians 6:12). Every time our fallen mind convinces us to bite the Devil's bait and hook, we're rendered ineffective in the fight. Don't be intoxicated by the allure of your mind's old ways of thinking. Be sober-minded about what's really happening around you. We're at war against an enemy that we're no match for. The more we have our minds disciplined to hear and obey the Holy Spirit within, the more we will walk in the victory that Christ has won for us.

Please, don't confuse this with the power of positive thinking mumbo jumbo that some teachers try to push on people. This is far beyond looking yourself in the mirror every morning and reciting positive words to yourself. Renewing the mind is a renovation of how you view the entire world in which you live. It's an entirely new way of thinking about everything. It's intentionally training your mind to be in sync with the mind of Christ through relationship with the Holy Spirit within you. It's filling your mind with God's thoughts – not your own – by internalizing the Scriptures. It's herding your thoughts through discipline and directing them toward godly ends. I'm not necessarily against positive thinking. I consider myself a positive person – sometimes to a fault. But positive thinking is no match for the fallen mind. The fallen mind will twist positive thinking into a means to attain its own selfish ambitions. Renewing the mind the way God has prescribed will lead you toward Christ-likeness and fulfilling kingdom-minded ambitions that God has planted in our new hearts.

When I played basketball, I used to give up a lot of shots, even easy ones at times. Sometimes it was a tactical error, but many times it was because I simply wasn't confident enough in my shot. As I got older, and more experienced, especially as an adult in city league, I began taking the philosophy – sometimes to my shame – that I'm going to miss every shot that I *don't* take. If you aren't engaging in renewing your fallen mind, you're a lot like I was in basketball: never taking shots, giving up easy baskets, never really contributing to the win. Renewing the mind is a challenging discipline, but then again, what is there about following Jesus that isn't a challenge?

Renew the mind. Get in the Word today. Start conversing with the Holy Spirit within you. Take your thoughts captive and redirect them towards those things that are true, honorable, pure, and praiseworthy. I promise you, the conflict within against this old body, against this old mind, is where the fight is at. And it's only through advancing in this fight that the new self – your new heart and new spirit – will gain opportunities to shine the light of Jesus into the darkness of this dying world.

References:
1. https://en.wikipedia.org/wiki/William_Tecumseh_Sherman
2. http://www.rjgeib.com/thoughts/sherman/sherman-to-burn-atlanta.html
3. http://www.medicaldaily.com/how-human-brain-works-brains-energy-efficiency-plan-maintains-electrical-charge-sustains-86b-neurons *If you have a hard time with evolution, forgive me. The science about the efficiency of the human brain is what's pertinent.*

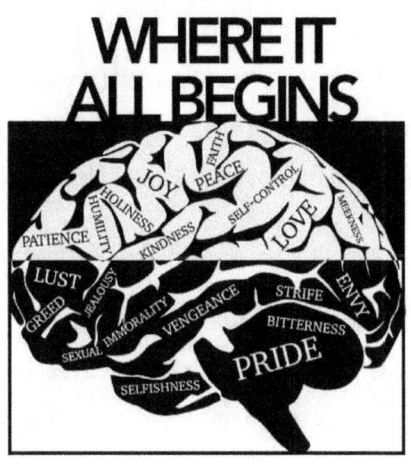

WHERE IT ALL BEGINS

The *shot heard round the world* is a phrase all Americans should be acquainted with. It refers to the first shot fired in the American Revolutionary war at Concord, Massachusetts. No one knows which side fired first, but when a shot is fired in the midst of armed, angry men, it doesn't matter who fired, the battle begins. What ultimately resulted from one, perhaps accidental gunshot, was an armed revolution of American colonists who would eventually win their independence from the British Empire. We can look back at history and see how it unfolded, what the results were, and trace the consequences of that first shot all the way up to the present.

Every battle has a first shot. Every consequence has a cause. The world seems designed to operate on a *cause and effect* paradigm. Every action, every word, bears a consequence; they produce fruit. The Bible keeps the metaphor for cause and effect in agricultural terms. Our choices bear fruit. And the fruit becomes a harvest. Therefore, when the time comes for harvest, the nature and quality of your fruit is what is key. You'll either reap good fruit, which leads to life, or you'll reap bad fruit, which leads to destruction.

> So, every healthy tree bears *good fruit,* but the diseased tree bears *bad fruit.* A healthy tree cannot bear bad fruit, nor can a diseased tree bear good fruit. (Matthew 7:17-18)
>
> I am the vine; you are the branches. Whoever abides in me and I in him, *he it is that bears much fruit,* for apart from me you can do nothing. (John 15:5)
>
> But now that you have been set free from sin and have become slaves of God, *the fruit* you get leads to sanctification and its end, eternal life. (Romans 6:22)
>
> Likewise, my brothers, you also have died to the law through the body of Christ, so that you may belong to another, to him who has been raised from the dead, in order that we may *bear fruit for God.* For while we were living in the flesh, our sinful passions, aroused by the law, were at work in our members to *bear fruit for death.* (Romans 7:4-5)

As I sit here writing, I am in my local McDonalds having a cup of coffee. The television on the wall is tuned in to the Today Show where they are discussing the new movies that will be hitting theaters during this Christmas season. The people around me are eating breakfast, talking with friends, and some are sitting with their spouses enjoying some laughs. The regular group of older gentlemen who are always in here *discussing* local issues, are a bit livelier today than other days. The employees are busy doing their routines. It's raining outside. I'm currently listening to some classical music in my headphones.

Everyone in this restaurant will make choices today that will bear fruit. The people on the Today Show are going to make choices that bear fruit. I am going to do the same. So will you. My choices today will bear fruit, which will later reap consequences. Those consequences will either give life, or they will bring destruction. And, those consequences will not only be limited to me, but they will give life or destruction to the people around me as well.

Choice. This is where it all begins. Our daily choices are what determine our harvest. Will it be a harvest of life, or a harvest of death? Timothy Keller told a story about how he became the pastor at Redeemer Presbyterian Church in New York City.[1] Keller and his wife planted Redeemer in NYC because they joined a Presbyterian denomination that encouraged church planting. They joined that denomination because in seminary Keller took two courses which convinced him that his theological leanings were Presbyterian. He was able to take those two courses because at the very last minute, his British professor, who was experiencing some bureaucratic difficulties with his visa, had those difficulties cleared up; this allowed him to legally come to the States and teach. The Dean of the school had been praying for this professor's issues to be cleared. The Dean's prayer partner was the son of President Gerald Ford (who was President at the time). Because his prayer partner was the son of the POTUS, strings got pulled and the professor's visa problems were cleared up. Gerald Ford was President because President Nixon resigned. President Nixon resigned because of the Watergate scandal. Watergate happened because the men who had broken in to the offices of the Democratic Party left the door unlatched. A security guard noticed the unlatched door, latched it, moved on, came back an hour later and noticed the door was unlatched again. He then called the police and everything about Watergate was discovered.

Because those operatives kept the door unlatched, Watergate happened, and things were set in motion that led to the planting of Redeemer Presbyterian Church in New York City. Choices matter. And God uses every one of them. The same choice that ruined the Presidency of Richard Nixon opened the door for thousands to be saved in NYC through the ministry of Timothy Keller at a church plant named Redeemer Presbyterian Church.

In the mid 1990s I was in college and I made *many* poor choices. One of those choices was to spend a third year at Northeast Mississippi Community College, which was technically a *two-year* college. It's not the third year itself that was a poor choice, it was my reasoning for taking a third year. See, had I done something like change my major, a third year might've been warranted. My reason was far more centered around a girlfriend than academics. A third year was uncovered by my scholarship. It became a financial burden on my parents. I had become irresponsible, *but I was in love*. I had grand plans, but as the relationship became increasingly dysfunctional, those plans dissolved. My third year at NEMCC increasingly seemed foolish.

But God was even using my foolish choices to bring about his plan for my life. During that year, I was encouraged to apply for a semester missionary position in Sterling, Colorado. It was essentially a ministry internship where I would assist Emmanuel Baptist Church in establishing a college ministry presence at Northeastern Junior College. I received that application around March of 1997, but I took it home and forgot about it. I literally didn't give it another thought because, in all honesty, I didn't feel like it was a fit. Sterling, Colorado was the last place I wanted to go.

As the spring semester of 1997 concluded, so did the relationship with my girlfriend of the last year and a half. That was the most tumultuous spring of my life (up until that point). I had been on an emotional roller coaster, I was starving spiritually, and I was desperately trying to find meaning and fulfillment in a relationship that was never going to work out. I had invested so much, I had made such a detour in my life plans to chase after her, only to fail.

I moved home from the dormitory. I was single, but more critically, I was jobless. I started looking for a job, but I was coming up with nothing. I interviewed a few times, but it always seemed to slip away. Finally, I was sitting at my desk in my bedroom, frustrated, in tears, crying out to God. "What am I supposed to do now?" In frustration, I swept my arms across my desk just to clear if off, and everything moved except one thing. I was looking down at that application for the position at Emmanuel Baptist Church. I may not be the sharpest knife in the drawer, but this seemed to be the bright neon sign that many of us have prayed for at times. I made a call to see if it was too late to apply. It was the *last day*. I filled out the application, delivered it that day, and started praying. About a week later, I received a phone call from a man named Stan Felder, who was the Missions Pastor at Emmanuel, and the rest is history. I moved to Colorado, served out the ministry, met my wife in the process, married her, and started our family.

The 1996-1997 school year may have been a year of foolish pursuits for me, but even in my poor choicess God was clearing a way to change my life forever. Let me be clear: from some of those poor choices I can still feel the ripples, and if I allow them they can be a source of unsteadiness in my walk. I'm just grateful to God that he took an opportunity to redeem that year of my life. Choices reverberate. They ripple. They echo. Whichever analogy you prefer, there's always an aftermath that you cannot anticipate. When you make choices remember that every choice is the beginning of a new series of consequences. Every choice is a new harvest of fruit.

> The heart of man plans his way, but the LORD establishes his steps. (Proverbs 16:9)

Does Keller owe a *thank you* to the guy who left that door unlatched at Watergate? Do I owe a *thank you* to my ex-girlfriend? No. At least not for getting us where we are today. God did those things. I'm sure the Watergate folks meant to conceal their presence a little better. In my heart, my plan going into that school year was to save up money, get a ring, get engaged, get married to my ex-girlfriend, then move to Hattiesburg, Mississippi and finish my degree at the University of Southern Mississippi. But that door at Watergate was found unlatched, and my own plans dissolved before my eyes so that God could unfold a greater plan, a greater purpose.

Everything begins with choice. There's a part of me that enjoys the endless discussion we could have about how God's sovereignty and man's choice work together. But for the purposes of this book, let's put it this way. The Bible teaches us that both are true. People are one hundred percent responsible for their choices *and* God's plan for the world is absolutely going to come about. Therefore, in accomplishing his own plans for bringing about the final fulfillment of his Kingdom on earth, God uses the free choices of men and women. This leaves our choices firmly in the category of free will, making us fully liable for whatever consequences result. This also leaves intact the sovereignty of God because he still accomplishes his ultimate will in redeeming both a Bride for Christ and all of creation for our eternal home.

Take a close look at your life. What you see can be placed in two broad categories. One category is the consequences of the choices you have made. These things are the fruit of you own choices. The other category is the consequences of the choices of others. The fruit of other people's decisions can take root in your life just as easy as the fruit of your own. How do we deal with each harvest? What can we do about our own choices? What can be done about the choices of other people? And how does God use them to accomplish his plan?

We should be careful here. We can oversimplify things to the point of saying that the condition of our lives is *simply* the result of our choices. That's horribly simplistic. Remember the Apostles? We might look at their lives and say that while they weren't perfect, they tended to make good, Spirit-led choices. And yet, all but one of them died martyr's deaths. Specifically, Paul was perhaps the most tortured of them all. Beaten, whipped, stoned, left for dead, shipwrecked twice, imprisoned, and yet he lived a spiritual life that we are encouraged to emulate. Godly choices don't guarantee comfort or a sparing from suffering. Sometimes bad choices lead to disaster. Sometimes *good* choices lead to disaster. The objective isn't to avoid disaster. The objective is to make choices that you know are in step with Jesus. Trouble *will* come. The question is whether it's coming by your own hand to destroy you, or by the hand of God to refine you.

We can also oversimplify things by saying that our lives are where they are because of the choices of other people. The choices of others indeed have their effect on us, but because our choices are ultimately still *ours,* blaming others for the consequences of our choices isn't an adequate defense. Take Samson as an example (see Judges chapter 16). Delilah, Samson's lover, was a Philistine spy. She tricked Samson into telling her the secret of his strength: his long hair. While he was sleeping, she cut it and had Philistine soldiers stand ready to take him. She woke him up, and the soldiers easily took him into custody because his strength was gone. Delilah sinned against Samson, but it was Samson's fault he was imprisoned by the Philistines. Had he married one of his own people (as the Law instructed) instead of having a mistress from an enemy of Israel, this would never have happened. Delilah was responsible, but Samson was more so.

The truth is, it's complicated. Our lives are a messy mix of consequences that result from our own doing *and* the doings of others. How in the world can we begin to get our minds around this mountain of choices that have shaped us into the people we are at this moment? For many of us, when we examine our lives we find ourselves in desolate places. Perhaps your own choices, along with the choices of others have landed you in a desperate place, spiritually, emotionally, physically, socially, and economically. And the worst part is that everything is spiraling out of control. Or maybe you're in the opposite place. You have everything you ever wanted. You've made good financial choices, you've made good career and family choices, you've taken care of yourself physically, but it all feels empty and all your *good* choices haven't given you any real peace or fulfillment. You're as desperate as the person on the other end of the spectrum whose experiences have been nothing like yours. Often the temptation is to lean toward the extremes of entirely blaming ourselves or other people.

The Bible teaches us something far more faceted, and complex. Because we are both sinners *and* people who are sinned against, who we are and the choices we make can't be boiled down into a simple formula. Take any family with two or more children as an example. Under normal circumstances what happens is you have parents who strive to raise each child under the same instruction, the same love, the same conditions. But the result is each child processes their rearing through different filters. None of the children come out the same. In fact, at times the children will take vastly different journeys. My sisters and I grew up with the same upbringing, but our journeys have been quite different. There is no formula, there is no guarantee in families that $a + b$ will always equal c. Our world is broken and our formulas, our ideas of how things should work out, are frequently sabotaged.

Who, or what, are the saboteurs of our choices? At times, we know the right choice, but we choose differently. What happens within that causes us to make a choice that we know is wrong? I've looked at myself in the mirror countless times and said, *why did I do that?* So have you. There's something at work within that steers us off course, even when we know it's the wrong direction. In Romans chapter seven, the Apostle Paul spells out his own internal struggle to help us understand what happens within us. Every born again person will contend with an internal struggle similar to what Paul describes. What he shares will shed some light on the process of our choices and why we are constantly looking in the mirror to say *why?*

The first saboteur is *sin* itself. We tend to think of sin as something we do, but less often do we think about sin being an influence or a force itself. Bear with me as I explain this. In a broken world, sin is like a force of nature. It affects everyone, it's impersonal, it doesn't play favorites, everyone is pulled and tugged by its influence and its effects. God himself even makes a reference to sin as a force that acts upon us.

> The Lord said to Cain, "Why are you angry, and why has your face fallen? If you do well, will you not be accepted? And if you do not do well, **sin is crouching at the door. Its desire is for you**, but you must rule over it." (Genesis 4:6-7)

Sin is more than just our actions, it's a force to be reckoned with that pulls us away from fellowship with God. It's no respecter of persons, it pulls on everyone from the Pope to the

Dalai Lama; the President to the CEO; suburbanites to the inner city; no one escapes its influence, no one is exempt from its effects. Even Jesus, who lived a sinless life, was affected – via other people's choices - by the power of sin around him.

Before I move ahead, Romans chapter seven is difficult to understand, partially because of Paul's writing style, but mainly because Christians can't seem to agree on how to interpret it. I'm going to give you my perspective on this, which isn't anything new, but understand that some scholars have a different point of view. I am not going to do a verse by verse breakdown of this chapter, but rather I want to draw out the big picture that Paul is illustrating of our internal struggle.

Romans 7:7-25 can be divided into two sections. The first is Paul explaining his life before Christ in verses 7-12, and the second is his description of life after conversion in verse 13-25. In the first section, Paul explains how sin used the Law against him. Paul, a Pharisee, well practiced on keeping the Law, could not keep himself from coveting. Coveting is an attitude of the heart, not an external action. Outwardly he wasn't a thief, he wasn't an adulterer, he wasn't a murderer, he honored his parents, he kept the Sabbath, he wasn't a liar, he worshiped no other Gods, he made no graven images, and he never used the name of the Lord in vain. But when it came to coveting, he could not gain the upper hand, and sin had him.[2]

> For sin, seizing an opportunity through the commandment, deceived me and through it killed me. (Romans 7:11)

Before Christ, I was never as pious as Paul. I had ongoing commandment issues with multiple commandments. I don't believe Paul meant to tell us that he was literally keeping all the commandments perfectly except the tenth one. But what he is saying is that the one commandment that consistently got him in trouble was coveting. And for all of us, sin takes advantage of God's law to make us sin even more. Here's what I mean.

If you're a parent, you'll understand this quickly. When your children were toddlers, they explored *everything*. They got into cupboards, they built elaborate ladders to climb up into cabinets, they dug things out of your closets, they had a natural curiosity about everything in your home. And once you caught them in a place where you didn't want them, you would tell them *no*. Right after the word *no* rolls off your tongue, a switch flips in the mind of the toddler. In a few cases – which to my knowledge and experience are urban legends – the child obeys and it's never a problem again. For most of us, the switch flips, and now the child is even more curious, even more determined to get into that forbidden place! Only, now they try to do it when you're not looking. In the child's mind, this place that was once an acceptable place to explore, is now forbidden and is *way more interesting*.

That's what sin does to us. The influence of sin's power actually increases our desire to disobey God's commands. The power of sin uses God's commandments to tempt our flesh to sin even more. Talk about a saboteur! We were born sinners because of Adam and Eve's choice. We're born in trouble. But on top of that, the power of sin capitalizes on our fallen state to cause us to sin even more because once we learn, *you shall not steal, you shall not commit adultery, etc.,* like toddlers our nature is to taste what has been forbidden. Sound familiar? Thank you, Adam and Eve!

In the second section (Romans 7:13-25), Paul shifts to his life with Christ. How do we know this? One reason is in the first section (7-12), he was writing in the past tense. From verse thirteen to the end of the chapter he writes in present tense. Paul describes an internal struggle between his new self's desire to love Jesus and follow his commands, and his flesh, which is still corrupted by the power of sin.

> For I know that nothing good dwells in me, *that is, in my flesh*. For I have the desire to do what is right, but not the ability to carry it out. For I do not do the good I want, but the evil I do not want is what I keep on doing. (Romans 7:18-19)

Notice he qualifies what he's saying: "nothing good dwells in me, *that is, in my flesh.*" This is the case for every believer. Every believer carries with them their new self and the Holy Spirit, which are *good*. But we also carry around with us a carcass of flesh that needs to be fed, that needs to be exercised, that needs to be given drink, but also that is completely corrupted by the power of sin. And because it is completely corrupted, it tends to turn these necessary things of food, drink, sex, etc., into addictions. Instead of being a means of survival, they become a means of soul satisfaction, which isn't their designed purpose. Herein is the struggle: the Holy Spirit builds up the new self, and the power of sin, through the flesh, tries to undo what the Holy Spirit is doing. This is how sin sabotages our choices: through appeals to our flesh. If the temptation is alluring enough, and if we haven't been in fellowship with Jesus enough, we will almost always make the wrong choice. No wonder Paul exclaims:

> Wretched man that I am! Who will deliver me from this *body of death*? (Romans 7:24)

I can relate to this cry! The times in my life where I have been most mired in disobedience are the most miserable times I can recall. For sure, you and I both are constantly dealing with disobedience. We all stumble in many ways (James 3:2), but there are the daily stumbles that we all contend with, then there are extended seasons of willful disobedience. I've had a few seasons, some longer than others, in my Christian walk where I was simply rebelling against following the Lord. Why? Because I thought I had a better plan. My plan made me feel good *right now*. God's plan was always deferring my satisfaction. My plan got me immediate results. God's plan was slower. I could connect the dots on my plan and somewhat predict what was going to happen. God only ever shows me the next step.

Confession time. My biggest trap is my own intellect. I'm not being arrogant when I say that I'm a smart guy. It's what many of my schoolmates remember me for. But I don't force my intelligence on people. I don't condescend. I've worked hard in my life to be relational and winsome with people so that I could be more than just a nerd. However, I do love diving into intellectual debate. Sometimes I get in over my head, but half the fun for me is working things out; finding the logic.

The downfall of being a smart guy is that it often leads to seasons of prayerlessness. I'm capable of creating and executing a plan with precision and with reasonably predictable results. If I'm not careful, I can operate from my intellect and leave the Holy Spirit out of the loop. Some of the longest periods of rebellion in my Christian walk weren't times of moral failure or drunkenness, but times of prayerlessness. When you aren't praying, you're not receiving direction. When you aren't praying, you're assuming you have things under control. When you aren't praying, you've essentially taken on the role of Master and Commander of your life. And when you are the Master and Commander of your life, in God's economy you can perhaps tread water for a short time, but eventually you find yourself far off course from where God would have you. At times, I've been dishonest. I've had bouts with lust. I've had rounds of anger and bitterness. But none of them compare to my extended battles of prayerlessness. My flesh, my fallen mind, the power of sin, they work against the Spirit of God within, convincing me that I've *got this*, when the reality is I've got nothing.

I am broken. Paul knew he was broken. That reveals the other saboteur of our choices: *our broken, fallen flesh*. I won't spend nearly as much time on this one because I think I've been clear. The power of sin can take advantage of us because our minds and our bodies – our flesh – are fundamentally corrupted. As I said in the last chapter, when Adam and Eve sinned, the connection they had with God, which sustained them spiritually and physically, was severed. At that moment, they suffered instant spiritual death, but physical death was a more gradual process. Disconnected from communion with God, the bodies he created for Adam and Eve began to slowly die. And every child born since then has been born spiritually dead and physically dying, just like their parents.

The choice of Adam and Eve set into motion every death, every temptation, every wicked act, every disease, every act of terrorism, every war that has happened since. Our flesh will always want to make choices that are contrary to God's desires. It doesn't know any other way. It is concerned primarily with its own satisfaction, period. Our thinking, from birth, is molded and shaped to fulfill the desires of our body as quickly and efficiently as possible.

Enter our choices. Because our thinking is conditioned for quick and efficient satisfaction of the body, our choices come from that thinking. As babies, we cry, we get whatever we want. As small children, we find out that crying doesn't always work, so we learn how to behave in certain ways to get what we want. As we mature, our behavior only gets more sophisticated, but its bottom line is still to get whatever it is we desire. Our whole life we make choices that work toward the goal of fulfilling our desires.

Enter the choices of others. Other people's choices affect us. Depending on what happens, if their choices work against us, we make a series of choices that serve to protect our interests. On the other hand, if their choices work for us, then we make different choices that springboards our progress toward our desires. But regardless, the bottom line is still that our choices always work toward fulfilling our desires.

Enter the new birth. When you are born again, suddenly you have new desires that are contrary to what your flesh wants. This is the internal struggle. Now you must choose which desires you will satisfy. This is a hallmark, a landmark, whatever you want to call it, of true conversion. *Internal struggle is a sign that you have a new self that wants to please Jesus rather than satisfying the desires of the flesh.* Choice suddenly takes on a new meaning. Where before you were simply choosing between which path would lead to the best satisfaction of your desires, now you are choosing between two masters. Will you choose to please Jesus, or please yourself?

If I could emphasize one thing it is this: the presence of internal struggle is a good thing. For a long time, I looked at it as a sign of failure, but now I see it as a sign of life! Because there's a struggle, it means there's life within me. Now my choices actually mean something more than just satisfying me, myself, and I. They have eternal impact. When I choose to follow Jesus, his kingdom will advance because I listened to him. But when I choose to follow the desires of my flesh, the only thing that grows is my appetite for more disobedience.

Don't for one second think that this is a fight between two equal forces. There is no yin or yang to the contest between the Holy Spirit and your flesh. He is greater! No contest. No debate. But he is also meek. He will not force you to choose his way. But rather through persuasion he convinces us to choose right. How does the Holy Spirit persuade us? Remember 2 Peter 1:3?

> His divine power has granted to us all things that pertain to life and godliness, *through the knowledge of him who called us* to his own glory and excellence, (2 Peter 1:3)

How has God appropriated his divine power to us for life and godliness? *Through our knowledge of Jesus!* It is through our understanding of Christ that the Holy Spirit convinces us that his way is better. All the power and authority that we receive as believers can only be as effective as our knowledge of

Christ is deep. Knowing Jesus unleashes the power we have been given. Knowledge isn't the goal. If knowledge is the goal, then you'll become arrogant. Knowledge isn't the power itself, but rather it unleashes the power you've been given in Christ.

Do your choices need to change? Learn of Christ. Increasing your understanding of Jesus will unleash divine power in your life that will lead to godly choices. In many ways, it's similar to how I have known my wife. When I married her, I loved her and knew her enough to know that I wanted no other. But as the years have passed, and I have known her deeper, my love for her is greater, and the lengths to which I would go to please her have increased exponentially. My choices are different simply because I love her. The same is true for Jesus. The deeper you know him, the more your love for him will increase, and the more your choices will be in line with his desires. Then the consequences of your choices, the fruit of your life, will turn from a harvest of destruction and death, to a harvest of life that benefits you, everyone you touch, and brings glory and praise to God. Your choice is where it all begins.

References:
1. Timothy Keller. Gospel in Life Podcast: *Does God Control Everything?* Published: December 2, 2010. http://www.gospelinlife.com
2. The concept that Paul wrestled with coveting comes from Timothy Keller's book, *Romans 1-7 For You*.

OUT WITH THE OLD

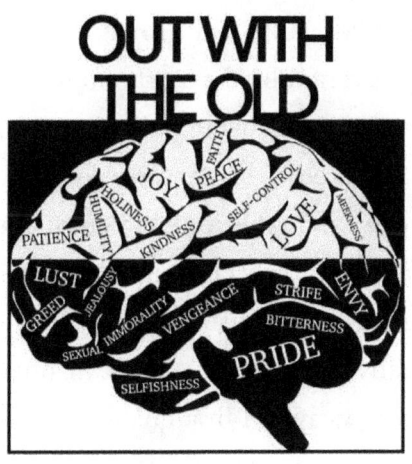

When I was a child, I was fascinated with my parents' closet. That closet was a treasure trove to me. It was a walk-in closet that had years of stuff stored on the shelves. It had become kind of the catch-all storage place in the house. If something didn't have a home, many times it landed in this closet. Games, old photo albums, boxes of 35mm slides, blankets, VHS tapes, cassettes, books, old maps, and to my child mind, that was the best room in the house. I even remember having dreams about that closet having a secret door that led to a hidden room in the house where there were even more treasures.

At some point in junior high, that bedroom became my bedroom, and that closet became my closet. By this time in my life, the magic of the closet had worn off. It wasn't my favorite room in the house anymore. It was just a closet with a bunch of unorganized stuff in it. In fact, as the years went on, the disorganized stuff had grown, and the closet space was shrinking. Eventually the stuff had to be reckoned with if I wanted to continue using this closet for its intended purpose. A slow process of cleaning and organizing began, and if you've ever done this, unless you're one of those *burn it all* kind of people, you sort through the stuff and determine what's trash and what's treasure.

Eventually it was done. As I recall, not nearly as much stuff was thrown away as I thought should happen. Instead what was needed most was some simple organizing, putting things in their own place, and making sure things remained in an organized state. Being a teenager, that wasn't top on my priority list, so this clean up happened several times while I occupied that room. But for sure, with each cleanup, there were things thrown away. Clutter happens when you live somewhere. Even if you're a neat person, you have places that accumulate the detritus of life. You only hide it better than others. Life makes messes, and occasionally those messes need to be cleaned up if you want to keep living.

A common thing that gets said about the Christian life is *come as you are*. I agree with that statement. You don't have to clean up your life to be reborn. The new birth happens in the middle of our debris. In fact, Jesus goes as far as to say that he didn't come for the healthy, but for the sick (Mark 2:17). He says that for two reasons. There are those who think they're healthy (but they're not) and they won't come to him because they don't see the need. If you think you're healthy you won't go to the doctor. Then there are those who know they are sick, and know they need healing. Therefore, don't bother cleaning your life up before you come to Jesus. He came for you just as you are. But also, if you did clean your life up before coming to Jesus you would become blind to your need for him because all would seem well. So, come as you are; don't wait, don't delay, just come, mess and all.

So you come. Now what? The most common misstep made after being born again is to *stay as you are*. By that I don't mean that you keep cheating, keep getting drunk, keep cussing . . . although some *professing* Christians keep doing those things. What I mean is you don't undergo a fundamental change in your core. You might change your outward behaviors, but truly, all it amounts to is a reshuffling of the deck. Instead of sexual conquest, you find other ways to be dominant. Instead of drinking away your stress, you eat your stress away. Your soul may be saved, but your life isn't fundamentally different because you're still handling your old problems with old solutions. If your reborn life is going to flourish, you must do more than simply reorganize the debris. There needs to be a clean sweep.

Think about it. What is the number one thing in your Christian walk that drags you back into the pit? It's the old ways of life; the old patterns of thinking; the old methods of problem solving; the old solutions for relieving the stresses of life; the old ways of resolving conflict; these are the things that pull us back into tangled webs of sin, guilt, and shame. There must be a constant, conscious effort to cast out our old ways if our spiritual lives are to bear any meaningful fruit for the kingdom of God. We should always be thinking and saying to ourselves, *out with the old, every day, in every way.*

My friend, John Stroup, runs a ministry in Springfield, Missouri called, Freeway Ministries. One of Freeway's missions is to offer the Gospel to addicts, and help those who receive Jesus to get clean and stay clean. I've visited their ministry, witnessed part of what they do, and it's obvious that God is working. John has been a guest at our church a few times, and on one of those occasions he said something that I've never forgotten. *The number one reason for relapse among recovering addicts is relationships.* Relationships often short circuit the recovery process. It's not because relationships are inherently bad, but it's because the greatest need during recovery – apart from Jesus Christ – is to lose dependence on a substance that is destroying your life. When you lose focus on the greatest need, even if you're tending to a good need, you still lose.

The typical scenario that plays out (and I've witnessed this) is two people meet in recovery group or treatment. They have a spark with each other and they chase that spark. Since neither of them are healthy in their minds yet, the relationship becomes the drug. The couple starts feeling fixed, they start feeling normal again because the attraction of the relationship is pumping them full of endorphins. Sometimes they drop out of recovery group, sometimes they don't, but in either case, when the initial relationship thrill is gone, they're both right back where they were before they met. No healing has happened, just pacification. And now that the relationship high isn't what it used to be, the craving returns with a vengeance. At this point, many relapse.

Just like drug addiction, this happens with all saved sinners. Christians are recovering sinners. And just like an addict needs to clean sweep their life in order to keep from relapse, Christians need a clean sweep to keep from falling back into their old ways of handling life. Your crowd will determine your crave. Whoever you surround yourself with will shape and mold your desires, your ambitions, and your direction. The Bible sums this up in one very short but powerful verse.

> Do not be deceived: "Bad company ruins good morals." (1 Corinthians 15:33)

I heard evangelist Ken Freeman put it a different way: *show me your friends and I'll show you your future.* The most important decision in life is to receive the gift of salvation offered in Jesus Christ. After that, your choice of peers is the second most important decision in your life. Your peers are who you emulate. They're who help you decide what is most important in this life. They're the pool of people from which you'll most likely meet your spouse. They'll be the ones who push you and motivate you. These things make the caliber of their character of utmost importance.

What does it look like for a person to clean house; out with the old? Is a believer supposed to just slough off their old friends like a snake sheds its skin? Are we supposed to abandon everything that was a part of our old life? That's a hard question to answer in black and white. The answer is always that we need to let go of anything that pulls us away from Christ, but most of us are poor judges of what we think we can handle. *That'll never tempt me. That'll never be an issue for me.* May I say, the moment you seriously think that about *whatever*, you have nearly consigned yourself to stumbling over *whatever*. No, we need to follow the examples of two men from the Word: Abraham and Moses.

Abraham, the father of many nations, is the father of the Jews and Christians by Isaac, and Arabs trace their lineage through his other son, Ishmael. Just a quick side note: this is the seed of all conflict between Muslims and Jews and Christians. Ishmael was born first, but he wasn't birthed by Abraham's wife, Sarah. Ishmael was birthed by Hagar, Sarah's handmaiden. However, God promised Abraham that his wife, Sarah, would bear a child, (Genesis 18:10) so Isaac was the son of promise, and the one who received the inheritance and the blessing.

To the point, Abraham shows us what it means to clean house. Before God called Abraham, he was living in a city called Haran. His family had migrated there from the city of Ur which is in modern day Iraq. In that day, Ur was the center of all moon worship in Babylonia, so it's a safe bet that Abraham's family was worshiping the moon, even after they moved to Haran. It's what they had been raised around, it's what they were taught. But one day, our Creator God spoke to him directly.

> Now the Lord said to Abram, "Go from your country and your kindred and your father's house to the land that I will show you." (Genesis 12:1)

Now the Lord said. As in all cases of salvation, God moved first. He called Abraham (his name was Abram until God changes it in Genesis 17:5). That's what happens to us. God calls us to salvation. Jesus teaches us in the Gospel of John that no one can be saved until he is first drawn by God (John 6:44). Salvation always begins with God making the first move. You didn't simply decide to be saved one day. God drew you in first.ABraham was going about life, loving his family, worshiping the moon, and then one day God spoke and called him. The God that perhaps he had heard of, the one that destroyed the world by flood, but spared his ancestor, Noah, and had been silent ever since. He just spoke. Suddenly the moon didn't seem to hold the power that it once did. Suddenly he knew that the one who created the moon had revealed himself. Suffice it to say, God had Abraham's attention, but more importantly, God had his heart.

Go from your country. The first command God issued to Abraham was get out. Leave the nation you have lived in for so long. Why? It was too familiar. Moon worship was something that Abraham had done his whole life. The culture to which he had grown accustomed was saturated with false religion. God knew that to transform Abraham into the father of many nations, he was going to have to get Abraham out of his normal experience. He had to get Abraham out of his bubble. Part of Abraham cleaning his house was to sweep out the idols that he had picked up from his peers in Ur and Haran. To do that, he had to leave because it was too easy to fall back into those false practices.

We are no different. Cleaning house means that we need to put ourselves in new surroundings. I'm not suggesting that it should be as extreme as Abraham. You don't necessarily need to leave the country. However, God *is* calling you to leave the things that entrap you. Abandon the things that are snares for you. Are you at a job that consistently puts you in situations where you sin? Get a new job. Do you live in a neighborhood that presents many temptations? Move to a new neighborhood. God's desire is for you to be transformed. If your surroundings are constantly booby trapping your spiritual growth, causing you to stumble again and again back into the things of your old life, *get new surroundings*. In many cases, it's easier said than done, but in all cases, it boils down to who you love more. Do you love Jesus more than the ease of staying where you are? God told Abraham to leave his country. Don't lose sight of how hard it is to move from somewhere you love. It might only take up a few words on the page of your Bible, but you can know for sure that leaving everything he had known and loved was one of the hardest things Abraham ever did. But he did it because God had captured his heart more than anything else.

Go from your kindred. The next thing was leave your family and friends. You and I know this is the hardest part of leaving. I've moved away from family and friends two times now. Once when I moved from my hometown in Mississippi to Colorado. The next time when I moved from Colorado to Missouri. Both times I was following the Lord's leading. Both times I was sure it was what God wanted. But both times, I left family and friends behind. Both times I started from scratch with building new relationships. In many ways I can understand Abraham's feelings in leaving behind all of the most important relationships in life. But for him, there was no Internet, no email, no Facebook; there wasn't even a postal service. When he left, he was leaving with the idea that he may never see or hear from these people again.

When we clean house, we must clean with the idea in mind that some of the relationships we have enjoyed may have to end. Why? Because, like we said earlier, relationships are the biggest reason for relapse. If your kindred are doing all the things that you're trying to leave behind, you need new kindred. All of Abraham's kindred were worshiping a moon god. God knew that the best way to do what he wanted to do in Abraham was to get him out of those relationships. Go from your kindred.

It's at this point that many objections get raised, the most common being about sharing the Gospel with our old friends. How can I share the Gospel with my old friends if I end the relationships I have with them? And don't you think ending the relationship is a bit harsh? Let's put it this way. Jesus said if your right hand causes you to sin, you should cut it off (Matthew 5:30). Sure, he's using a metaphor, but the implication is that we need to deal severely with the things in our lives that drag us back into sin. If you have family and friends that keep dragging you back into sin, you must cut them off. Now this isn't to say that you're burning your bridges with people, but make a graceful exit so that one day, if the Lord leads, you still have an inroad with them to share the light of the Gospel. This is, without doubt, one of the hardest parts of being a disciple of Jesus. Losing friends and family for the sake of pursuing Jesus will be always be hard to endure. But he promises us that whatever we've lost in terms of those relationships, we will regain them a hundredfold.

> And everyone who has left houses or brothers or sisters or father or mother or children or lands, for my name's sake, will receive a hundredfold and will inherit eternal life. (Matthew 19:29)

I can speak of this personally. In 1997, when I moved to Colorado, I had just barely turned twenty-one years old. I knew that Jesus was calling me to move, so I moved there with the intentions of only being there for the school year, which was the length of the ministry internship I had applied for. I moved in August, and I intended to return home in

May. But the longer I was there, the more I began to understand that this wasn't going to be a nine month stay. And these thoughts were occurring to me before I met Radene. I left my family. I left my friends. To say that the culture in Colorado was different from Mississippi is understating the case. I felt like I was learning a whole new set of customs, expressions, and expectations. For a while I felt like the proverbial fish out of water. There were indeed lonely times where I missed my friends and family.

But as I remained faithful to what God had called me to do, he began planting people in my life that became incredible friends, even to this day. I gained a new family when Radene and I became serious about marriage. Can I be honest? I have life-long relationships from Mississippi, but I have the deepest relationships in Colorado, and now, Missouri. Jesus promises us that those things we lose for His name's sake will be restored a hundredfold. I have experienced this; I believe it with all my heart. And it doesn't cause me to be careless in ending relationships simply because he promises to replace them, but instead it gives me peace when it actually does come down to parting ways with someone. Parting ways isn't easy, but it's only our arrogance and desire for control that insists we must remain a part of someone's life. If you feel like you can't part from someone because you must be a light in their life, that's not love. That's codependency. God is their sufficiency, not you. Had Abraham refused to leave and told God that there's many people in Haran who need saving that he could witness to,

God might've just found another guy. And Abraham would've been remembered . . . well, he wouldn't be remembered at all. Cleaning house means we can't continue in the same company we always had.

Go until I say stop. It should be noted that God didn't tell Abraham where he was going. He said *go to the land I will show you.* If you have control issues, this is the worst. If you are one of those people who need to have things mapped out before you'll make a move, you'll have difficulty following Jesus. God seldom tells us exactly what's coming. I've had several moments in life where I know God gave me a head's up that something is coming, but he never told me exactly what it would be. That's not to say that God never does this. In fact, one of the things Jesus told us the Holy Spirit would do is reveal things to come (John 16:13), and I believe he can do this through the spiritual gifts he gives to us.

But to put things in perspective there are sixteen prophets in the Old Testament, and three believers in the New Testament whom we can say for sure that God gave them specific, detailed revelations about future events. Out of many thousands upon thousands upon thousands of God's children from Abraham to the Apostle John, only nineteen are recorded to have had detailed and specific prophecies about the future. Most of us live like Abraham, trusting and depending on the Lord for each step until we arrive where he wants us to be because God wants our relationship with him to be based on unshakable faith, not empirical certainty.

[And let's be honest. For many of us, when we hear someone say they've received a "word" from God about what's about to happen, we groan inwardly because it feels like a report from the tabloid section that claims to have new predictions from Nostradamus. Is it right to feel like that automatically? Probably not, but there have been so many fakes, so many books written by charlatans; (Anyone remember *88 Reasons Why the Rapture Will Be in 1988*?) it's no wonder that many of us are jaded and cynical when it comes to self-proclaimed prophets.]

In one sense, we all know where God is leading us. He's leading us to a transformed life that thinks like, speaks like, lives like Jesus Christ. In one sense, we all know that the final destination is an Earth where Heaven has literally came down and God dwells among his people in eternal harmony and bliss. But in the meantime, our journey is seldom mapped, and it takes us to places that we could never have predicted when we began. My plan for life at age twenty-one looks nothing like where I am today. I was a Social Sciences major and my plan was to teach high school and coach basketball somewhere in Northeast Mississippi. Today I'm a worship pastor, photographer, podcaster, and author with a Bachelor of Science in Organizational Management in Christian Leadership. Oh, and I've now lived in three different states.

Abraham's plan probably didn't include following God on an adventure to an unknown place. But in faith, he followed God until he was told to stop and settle. The Word says that Abraham's faith was counted to him as righteousness (Genesis 15:6). Some of us have tried cleaning house, but we've tried to do so on our own terms and in our own wisdom, and while things might've been better for a while, we ultimately fall back into the pit. *There's no faith involved in cleaning house your way.* There's no righteousness, no reward to be gained from trusting yourself. In faith, go from your country and your kindred on a journey that God will take you through step by step.

In the last couple of years, I've attempted to counsel a few people through some difficult times in their lives. One of them grew up in church. He has godly parents, but slowly he rejected their hopes for him and carved out his own path. He ended up getting a girl pregnant, marrying her, but discovering after they married that she was pretty messed up (so was he by this time). I counseled him.

I counseled him.

I counseled him.

Finally, one day, while he and I were having lunch, I got plain with him. I told him that he's ignored everything I've shared with him and had followed his own counsel, his own wisdom, and it had done nothing but dig his hole deeper. Then I said this: "When will you realize that your wisdom really kind of sucks?" He hasn't reached out to me since. Perhaps I should've said it nicer. Regardless, to my knowledge, he's still finding out how deep the rabbit hole goes. But the truth is, we're all kind of thick. We've all tried sweeping our houses clean the way we think is best without consulting the Lord. Eventually you discover that you're not as wise or as clever as you thought because you find out that nothing has changed; you've only rearranged the mess.

So there's the example of Abraham who shows us how to leave behind everything that hinders us. Moses presents us with a different perspective on what it means to clean house. Thanks to Hollywood, many of us have received certain glimpses into the life of Moses without even reading the Bible. Some of them have been better than others, but the common thread that they all nailed was that Moses was born into slavery as a Hebrew, received into Pharaoh's family as an infant, and raised as a royal (see Exodus 2:1-10). However, not much is said about Moses' youth and young adult years, which is where Hollywood has taken much license. Here's what we know for sure.

> When the child grew older, she [Moses' mother] brought him to Pharaoh's daughter, and he became her son. She named him Moses, "Because," she said, "I drew him out of the water." One day, when Moses had grown up, he went out to his people and looked on their burdens, and he saw an Egyptian beating a Hebrew, one of his people. (Exodus 2:10-11)

In those two verses, it is believed there is a lapse of forty years. Let me draw this out for you. In God's providence, when Pharaoh's daughter found Moses in the water, God worked it out so that Moses' mother, Jochebed, became his nursemaid. Jochebed nursed him and raised him, teaching him about being a Hebrew and their family history, probably until the age of twelve. Then she brought him to Pharaoh's daughter, where he began receiving instruction and training in how to rule and govern Egypt as a royal. That's all contained in verse ten. Skip forward about twenty-eight years, then you arrive in verse eleven.

For most of Moses' life, he lived as a royal. He was respected as a royal. He enjoyed the riches of Pharaoh's house. But all along, he never forgot what his mother taught him about being a Hebrew. He never forgot his heritage as a son of Abraham, Isaac, and Jacob. Much of Moses' adult life sounds kind of like the typical American Christian. We are rich. Compared to our brothers and sisters throughout history, and compared to many of them around the world in the present, we enjoy a comfortable life. We have been living in Pharaoh's house, benefiting from being a citizen of his family, even as we are aware of the suffering that many of our kindred have endured, and are presently enduring.

Moses then encounters an Egyptian beating a Hebrew. In that moment, he encountered a crisis of belief in his heart. Who is he really? Was he an Egyptian or a Hebrew? Was he going to ignore this injustice and continue enjoying his privilege as a citizen of Pharaoh's house, or was he going to embrace who he really was, a Hebrew, and stick his neck out for his brother?

He looked this way and that, and seeing no one, he struck down the Egyptian and hid him in the sand. (Exodus 2:12)

Was murder the answer? No, but his decision to embrace his Hebrew heritage cost him his Egyptian citizenship because it became known among the slaves that he had killed an Egyptian officer. He fled Egypt for fear of being caught and put to death himself. I can't condone murder, but his decision to side with his oppressed brothers was the right thing to do. Christians, especially those of us in comfy western nations, the day has come where we must do what we can to side with our oppressed brothers, even if it costs us our citizenship in Pharaoh's house. We must be willing to lose our comforts, lose our reputation, lose our freedoms, no matter what the cost, to side with the oppressed of God's family.

Around the world, even in our own nation, God's people are oppressed, ridiculed, persecuted, marginalized, and many of us refuse to side with them because it would mean losing something. Losing friends, losing respect among peers, losing liberties, losing dignity; we are too afraid to be uncomfortable and unpopular. This is to our shame.

Cleaning house means losing more than friends, more than possessions: it means losing yourself. It's not done all at once, but rather it's a daily affair of casting out the old. Every day is a new opportunity for your flesh to reassert itself. The

Apostle Paul knew this, and he wrote this to Roman Christians.

> So you also must consider yourselves dead to sin and alive to God in Christ Jesus.Let not sin therefore reign in your mortal body, to make you obey its passions. Do not present your members to sin as instruments for unrighteousness, but present yourselves to God as those who have been brought from death to life, and your members to God as instruments for righteousness. For sin will have no dominion over you, since you are not under law but under grace. (Romans 6:11-14)

Since the power of sin is an active force to be reckoned with, and our fallen flesh is primed to give in to it, we must do what we can to give ourselves the advantage in this conflict. There is an active resistance in which every believer must engage. Make a conscious choice every day that sin will not have authority over your body. When Paul says don't present your members to sin, that very literally means you should protect your hands, your feet, your ears, your lips, and any other body part from being used to sin's advantage. If you've ever heard someone say *you're dead to me*, that's what Paul is saying we should tell ourselves about sin every day. You're dead to sin, so stop allowing it to dominate your mind and body.

I've made no secret of the fact that there was a time in my life where I allowed pornography to dominate me. And if you ever get into a group of honest men, most of them will tell you the same thing. Of course, unless you have the Holy Spirit within telling you this is wrong, you won't really see yourself as being dominated. It just seems natural and normal because God has designed men to enjoy the sight of beautiful women. But when you are born again, suddenly you have a voice within telling you that you shouldn't let your eyes look at such things. It's not the voice of your mother (although that's a voice men frequently hear in their head), but it's the voice of God speaking truth to your new self. The Holy Spirit is *a person*. Theologically we call him the third person of the Trinity. And as a person, he desires that you and I cultivate a friendship with him.

Every day I must consciously choose that this day I will listen to the voice of the Holy Spirit when it comes to where I allow my eyes to drift, and what I allow my mind to dwell upon. Folks, I've fought this for too long to be anything less than honest here. If I don't consciously choose each day – even each moment – to give the Holy Spirit control over this, the power of sin will do its best to lead my eyes and my mind astray. Pornography creates a well-worn groove in the mind (so does any addiction for that matter) kind of like the gutter on a bowling lane. Once the ball falls into the gutter, it's almost a sure bet that because of its momentum it's going to stay in there until it hits the wall behind the pins at the end of the lane.

My advice? Just don't go bowling. But unfortunately, that's what we frequently do. We put ourselves in places and situations where we can throw a gutter ball, even though it's never our intention. If you want to stay out of the gutter, the only way you can guarantee you don't throw a gutter ball, is to not bowl at all. Even pros fall in the gutter on occasion.

Cleaning house, casting out the old, considering yourself dead to sin, this is what we must do if Jesus is to truly have reign in our lives. But this is only half of our discipline. What remains to be done when we cast out the old is a work unto itself, and it deserves a chapter of its own.

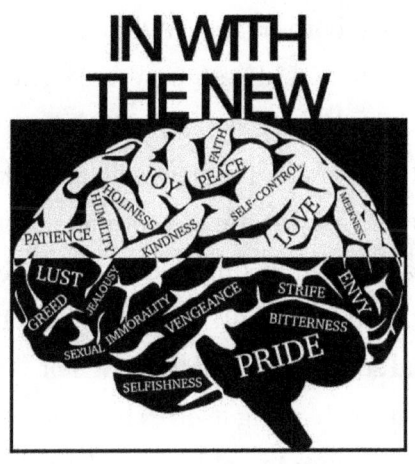

This is the middle. This is the innermost part. You are now in the most inner chapter of this book. There are equal numbers of chapters on either side. So far, we've delved into the reality that we are in a spiritual battle at all times, that our choices are where it all begins, and that our old self, the old ways of thinking and living, are things that we must put out of our lives. I didn't consciously plan it this way, but here at the middle, we need to have a conversation about the new you. Paul calls it your *inner* self.

> So we do not lose heart. Though our outer self is wasting away, our inner self is being renewed day by day. (2 Corinthians 4:16)

This inner self is the new you that was brought to life the day you were born again. We just had a conversation about putting out the old self; a necessary, daily discipline that must be done if the new self is to mature and flourish. Maturing and nourishing the new self, is a work unto itself. You can't simply cast out the old to make room for the new and expect the new self to simply occupy those empty places automatically. And if I didn't say it before, I'll say it now: denying the old self *is* a work of the new self. The old self will never participate in denying itself. The new self must actively engage in making sure the old self is denied at all points of entry. But I think before we can wrap our minds around the monumental discipline that falls upon the new self, you and I need to understand the nature of the new self. Who is it? What is its desires? Where does its power come from? How do we nurture it? How can it flourish? All these questions are important to understand if you are to know *who* is in your middle.

I'm no expert in this field, but I've noticed many of the youth that have grown up around me, including my own kids, are profoundly impacted by the four years that cover fifth to eighth grades. It's in those years where they enter puberty, their bodies change, and they typically find their pack of friends that they'll stick with all through high school. Social roles are defined. The bullies, the jocks, the preps, the nerds, and whatever other social categories that we can define today, they're all assigned concretely during these four years.

And with little deviation, these paths are followed through till the end of their school career.

Are there exceptions? Of course, but for the most part once a kid falls into a social track, peer pressure, peer expectations, and the momentum those things create will keep a kid in the role he or she picks up during those fifth to eighth grade years. Some people embrace those roles because popularity comes as part of the package. Some people try desperately to break out of their role because it brings a stigma. But the social inertia of middle school often carries through high school. At times it also carries into adulthood. Sometimes it changes. But without exception, your teen experiences usually stay with you your whole life because there's so many firsts: first time driving a car, first date, first kiss, first job. Our firsts are burned into our memory because they're almost always associated with strong emotions. If you were blessed to have healthy firsts, then you won't feel stigmatized entering adulthood, and that gives you an emotional head start. But head start or not, it's our early experiences that shape us the most. They lay the foundation for the rest of our lives. Identity springs from here.

Who we are is a complicated issue. Genetics, environment, circumstances, a combination of these things define us. In some ways, you can say that these things determine us. Yes, we make our own choices, but our choices are inevitably made because of the influence of genetics, environment, and circumstances. They don't make them for us, but they certainly persuade us to choose a particular way, which is why what I wrote in the previous chapter is so important.

I know a young man whose life, so far, has been rocked by trouble upon trouble. He has extended family that loves him dearly, but his immediate family has been one long story of disaster upon trouble upon tragedy. No stability. No foundation. Now he lives his life hand to mouth. Everything is survival. No foresight, no planning, only where can I make the next dollar to get the next thing I need to survive. Despite his extended family's efforts to help and their attempts to reason, he's making decisions that line up with what he has learned from his upbringing and jive with the influence of his peers; and so does everyone else.

Until Jesus.

Salvation births a new inner self, the new self, the new you. He's a person who's never existed before until the moment you were saved. Your new self needs an introduction. Who is your new self? First, your new self still looks like you. You aren't going to look in the mirror and see a new face. Your new self still has the base of experiences and knowledge you've always had. It's still you, but it's a new you.

If you've been around long enough to experience a ten year reunion of your graduating class, you can probably relate to this. My ten year reunion was in June of 2004. We didn't have a large senior class. We topped out at thirty six. Our school was small, and in a small town. Unlike my wife, who had well over a hundred in her senior class, I knew *everyone* in my class. I don't know if everyone feels this way (probably not) but between seventeen and twenty-seven, I had become a totally new person. I was still growing, but God had done a transformation in me during those ten years, and the person I was in high school seemed like a distant bad dream.

We had a barbeque at a classmate's home. It was fun. But it was also kind of weird. In my naivety, I thought everyone had been on a similar life-changing journey. But when we all got back together, it kind of just felt like old times. Everyone fell back into their high school roles. The same people talked. The same people sat together. And to some extent, it seemed we all were okay with it... except me. I was desperate for someone to notice that I had changed, but I wasn't going to be obnoxious about it. I was going to play it cool and wait for someone to ask about my life and just kind of reveal things naturally. Well, that never happened. I mean I talked with people, but it never felt *natural* to just blurt out how much better my life was than it was ten years ago. And so after three or four hours, the reunion ran its course and we all went our separate ways again for another ten years.

Hence the need for your new self's introduction. The natural course of things will never give an opportunity for your new self to have its coming out party. The new self must be displayed intentionally. Who is your new self? Colossians chapter three is one of the best places to go for learning about your new self. In fact, almost immediately the Lord is telling us that the new self is all about being intentional.

> If then you have been raised with Christ, seek the things that are above, where Christ is, seated at the right hand of God. Set your minds on things that are above, not on things that are on earth. For you have died, and your life is hidden with Christ in God. When Christ who is your life appears, then you also will appear with him in glory. (Colossians 3:1-4)

Seek is a directive. *Set* is a directive. *Seek* the things that are above, *set* your minds on things that are above; both are saying the same thing. Getting to know the new self begins with resetting the focus of your mind. You may be born again, but as we've said already, your mind needs to undergo a renovation; which is why we spent so much time discussing what needs to be cast out in the previous chapter. *Here's where we start replacing what we've expelled.*

I wish I had an amazing personal testimony about this. I wish I could sit here and tell you that my life has been one bright, shining, living example of laser like focus on Jesus. But the truth is most of my Christian life has been a cycle of focus and distraction, focus and distraction. The greatest times of focus in my life are frequently followed with a season of distraction. Being in ministry isn't an insulator from distraction. I would testify that the distractions one can encounter in ministry are far more insidious. They look good, in fact sometimes they look great and seem like worthy causes for your time, but in the end they only pull you away from intimacy with God. These kinds of distractions consume your time in ways that sap your personal time with Jesus. Let me give you one example.

I came to a point in my ministry where the only time I was reading the Word was when I was preparing for a study or a sermon. If you're a teacher or preacher, you know that preparation is a big part of your ministry. I'm not the primary preaching pastor at our church, but I do teach a couple times a week in small groups, and occasionally I preach. Prep for two studies often takes a lot of time. At one point, I had justified in my mind that I was reading the Bible all the time, so if I didn't read it first thing in the morning, I would get to it later. This was a trap for me because, quite frankly, I'm not a morning person; it doesn't take much for me to justify getting up at six thirty instead of five o'clock.

Gradually I found myself spiritually fatigued. I was even losing motivation to prepare for the studies I was leading, not because I thought it unimportant, but rather I found that the focus for my calling was waning along with my personal devotion. I would get distracted with other things. Fixing things. Upgrading things. Going places. Overcommitting myself. My schedule would fill up with things that kept me busy, which maintained an appearance of godliness, but it wasn't nourishing me spiritually.

> For to set the mind on the flesh is death, but to set the mind on the Spirit is life and peace. (Romans 8:6)

I wasn't physically dying from what I was doing, but my spiritual life was suffocating. Death comes to those who keep their mind set on the flesh. I was letting ninety minutes of sleep suffocate me spiritually. And the thing about spiritual suffocation is that it never stops with the spirit. What you sow in the spirit will eventually grow physical fruit. So my come to Jesus moment was when this began growing some visible fruit in my life. I was getting short with my family. My annoyance wasn't hard to surface. I was easily angered, which isn't who God has been recreating me to be. My brother-in-law, Casey, told me recently that I'm unflappable, which wasn't the case before I knew Jesus. God has grown a level-headed spirit within me that goes contrary to who I once was. When Radene and I first married, I was a yeller, but today I'm more collected than she is sometimes. I don't say this to embarrass her, or highlight any weakness in her, but to point out how God has transformed my character over the years. I know something is amiss when that level-headed spirit in my life goes missing. To my shame, it's usually pointed out to me by one of my children.

Seek the things that are above. Then it goes on to say something really important that we often miss. *Your life is hidden with Christ in God.* Why keep your focus on the things that are above? Because the source of our new life is with Christ, in God. If you aren't intentionally seeking the things above, from where your new life is sourced, you'll be disconnected from the very thing that will nourish your new self, leaving you only with the passions and lusts of your flesh to guide you. The new self is intentional about growth and remaining connected to its source of life, hidden in Christ.

> Do not lie to one another, seeing that you have put off the old self with its practices and have put on the new self, which is being renewed in knowledge after the image of its creator. Here there is not Greek and Jew, circumcised and uncircumcised, barbarian, Scythian, slave, free; but Christ is all, and in all. (Colossians 3:9-11)

See the intentional nature here? You work to put off the old self, on purpose: out with the old. Then there's the work of putting on the new self. It doesn't happen automatically, it must be purposefully pursued. Some might conclude this sounds an awful lot like a works based salvation. What happened to Jesus' yoke being easy and his burden being light? I hear that question, and I acknowledge that the church hasn't always done a good job of teaching through this issue. Let me put it this way. It's the difference between salvation and sanctification; between getting saved and living saved. You can't be good enough to earn salvation. There are no works that will save you, and likewise, there are no works that will keep you saved. Jesus has done the heavy lifting of qualifying us for heaven by being our substitute on the cross. He qualifies us, and he keeps us qualified.

But living saved, the sanctification of our life, that takes work. And if you're really saved, it's a work you'll gladly do because of the great love you have for Jesus. Jesus' statement, *if you love me, you'll keep my commandments* (John 14:15) is the tell all verse for what true love for Jesus looks like. Jesus never told us there wouldn't be hard work in the born again life. He has only promised us that he will give us the power to do it through the Holy Spirit. And herein is the secret.

If you go on your own quest to put off the old self and put on the new self, you'll eventually fail miserably from fatigue and weariness. But, if you are waiting for the Holy Spirit to instruct you in what you should do and how you should do it, his power will sustain you in the execution. This is where the Word of God becomes radically important. You will find ninety percent of your instruction already written out for you, and the Holy Spirit will empower you do these. The other ten percent of instruction comes in listening in the moment, listening in your prayer life, and listening to the Body of Christ.

Listening in the moment is a learned, acquired skill. You must train yourself to *pray without ceasing*. Our minds are pre-programmed to evaluate, plan, and overcome the obstacles of each day. We do it without thinking. Our minds are always processing information. The discipline of unceasing prayer isn't literally staying locked up and on your knees in your prayer closet. It's the skill acquired from retraining your mind to pray before processing. Before immediately drawing conclusions based on what you're seeing, you filter what you see through an internal conversation with the Holy Spirit. Then your actions are rooted in that conversation. This isn't convenient. It takes time, and sometimes it means holding your tongue until you receive instruction on what to say. Then, there are times where situations demand quick responses that don't necessarily give you time for a pause to pray. If you've been renewing your mind in the Word, *that* is the ammunition the Holy Spirit uses for those quick-draw and fire moments.

Listening in prayer is another thing that we don't do naturally. Either through bad modeling or bad teaching or both, we learn to monologue in prayer. We enter our prayer closet, and engage in a one-sided conversation where we do all the talking. For sure, God does want us to talk. He wants us to praise him, he wants us to confess, he wants us to make our requests, but he also wants us to *be still*.

> Be still before the Lord and wait patiently for him; (Psalm 37:7)

Some translations say, *be silent before the Lord*. Stillness and quiet before the Lord gives you an opportunity to hear him speak. That comes from reading the Word, but it also comes from listening for the voice of the Holy Spirit. He will speak to you. But if you're doing all the talking, he won't get a word in edgewise.

There are so many examples from my life that I could give you, but one of my favorite things is from the movie, *The Incredibles*. The villain, Syndrome, has captured Mr.

Incredible, who is the strongest man alive. He has him cornered in the jungle with a machine that he designed especially for capturing Mr. Incredible. While he's cornered, Syndrome begins waxing eloquently on how he used to look up to Mr. Incredible, but has out grown him, and how he will now become the world's hero without superpowers, but with his own inventions. While Syndrome is giving his monologue, Mr. Incredible is slowly edging his way over toward a large tree trunk, which after a few moments he picks up and throws at Syndrome. Syndrome dodges, incapacitates him with one of his inventions, and says, "You sly dog, you got me monologuing! I can't believe it!"[1] I love that movie, and the point is, we're like Syndrome. The Holy Spirit is trying to say something, but we're too wrapped up in our monologue to notice.

Then there's listening to the Body of Christ, which may be the hardest of the three because it requires more discernment. The Holy Spirit is present in all believers, and he has given us apostles, prophets, evangelists, pastors, and teachers (Ephesians 4:11) whom we would usually have little problem receiving instruction from. But here's where it gets a little more uncomfortable for many of us. Since the Holy Spirit is present in all believers, he can use *any* believer to speak to us. As we are being *renewed in knowledge after the image of our creator*, we become conduits for the Holy Spirit to work through us to impact other people for the kingdom. You *will* be used to speak truth into someone else's life if you keep listening to the Holy Spirit and follow his lead in your daily life.

We can get a little testy when people come to us and offer advice or instruction, even a little correction. I know some people who won't believe it unless it comes from a pastor, or it even must come from the *right* pastor. But in Christ the gifts and roles of responsibility in the church aren't meant to be dividing lines between those who know, and those who don't, and therefore those whom we listen to, and those we don't (although there is wisdom in obtaining the input of those whose ministry is to study and teach the Word). In Christ, *there is not Greek and Jew . . . slave or free; but Christ is all, and in all.* If he is in all, then *any* believer can be a messenger. You only need to discern whether what's being said is for you, from the Lord, through this person speaking to you. That takes discipline as well.

I've had this very thing happen to me, many times. When people come up to me and say they have a *word* for me, I'm always interested in what they have to say. I'm not afraid of people prophesying to me, and I'm not afraid to call out so-called prophets when they get out of line with the Gospel. You don't have to be afraid either. If it's from the Lord, first it will agree with the Bible. If a person comes to you and says they have a word from God, but then tells you something that goes against the written Word of God, you can dismiss what that person says, and if you have opportunity, offer correction to them. Second, it will testify with the Holy Spirit within you. In other words, if someone prophesies to you, the Holy

Spirit within will tell you if this is true or not. Every person who offers you a word from God, a prophecy, whatever you want to call it, they must be consistent with the written Word, and the testimony of the Holy Spirit within you. If either of them fail, then it's not for you. If it passes the tests of Scripture and the Holy Spirit, then, and only then, will it be valid. This is called *testing the spirits to see if they're from God.*

> Beloved, do not believe every spirit, but test the spirits to see whether they are from God, for many false prophets have gone out into the world. (1 John 4:1)

Back in the 1990s, during my college days, I was at a Bible study with a group of friends. The leader of the group had invited someone in to teach about spiritual warfare. In my church background there was very little talk about this subject – or maybe I wasn't listening. Regardless, I was interested. I honestly don't remember the study very well because what happened at the end of it superseded everything else. At the end of the study, the leader had each of us stand up in a line. I had no idea what was coming, so I made sure I wasn't first in line. He started at the end of the line on my right, and began praying over each person, and for each person he had a prophecy. I'm kind of interested in this, but at the same time, this was one of the guys my church warned me about. False prophets. Emotionalism. False tongues. Those words were bubbling up from my background. They weren't mean spirited, but they were firm, strong warnings.

But as I listened, none of those descriptions seemed to fit this guy. He wasn't speaking in tongues, he wasn't trying to elicit a response from us through emotional appeals, but rather he was praying over us, and then grabbing us by the shoulders, looking us in the eyes and offering a word of knowledge, encouragement, and yes, for some of us, a prophecy. So by the time he arrived to me, I was eager to hear what he had to say. He prayed, then he looked me in the eyes and said, "You're a man after God's own heart," three times and then added, "and children will be hanging from your arms and strengthened."

I can't explain it to you, but in that moment, I broke. I wept. I don't know why. I didn't even really like kids. Maybe the thought of it upset me. But the night ended, and I went back to my dorm room encouraged. In the days that followed there were questions and disagreements over the things this man taught us, and how he prayed overs us. I didn't really care about that. I just knew that something broke in me, and I sensed a freedom that I hadn't known.

That next summer, I spent eight weeks living on a Boys Ranch as a summer missionary. And as I played in the swimming pool with the kids one day, they were climbing all over me, and that prophecy came back to mind. If I had been alone, I would've probably cried all over again, but my back was about to break from the weight of these kids crawling on me. I'll never forget that day. God taught me that he can speak to me through other believers. And besides, is it not through other believers that we even have a Bible? You see, almost always, God has spoken to us through other faithful believers. The question is can you accept that he can speak to you through *anyone* he chooses?

If you can wait upon the Lord to give you instruction, first from the Word, then listening to him in the moment, in your prayer closet, and in the Body of Christ, then your new self will be fully equipped for anything the world can throw at you. The new self is already pre-loaded with desires to please God. Therefore, by renewing your mind in the Word, and listening to the Holy Spirit, you are giving your new self the necessary ammunition for spiritual battle.

I've spent a lot of time in this chapter talking about the disciplines of seeking and listening, and for good reason. These comprise the vast majority of the battle to nourish your new self. But how do you know if you're making progress in renewing your inner man? Keep reading in Colossians chapter three.

> Put on then, as God's chosen ones, holy and beloved, compassionate hearts, kindness, humility, meekness, and patience, bearing with one another and, if one has a complaint against another, forgiving each other; as the Lord has forgiven you, so you also must forgive. And above all these put on love, which binds everything together in perfect harmony. And let the peace of Christ rule in your hearts, to which indeed

you were called in one body. And be thankful. Let the word of Christ dwell in you richly, teaching and admonishing one another in all wisdom, singing psalms and hymns and spiritual songs, with thankfulness in your hearts to God. And whatever you do, in word or deed, do everything in the name of the Lord Jesus, giving thanks to God the Father through him. (Colossians 3:12-17)

Compassionate hearts, kindness, humility, meekness, patience, forgiveness, love, peace, gratitude, accountability (teaching and admonishing), wisdom, joy (psalms, hymns, spiritual songs), and steadfastness (doing everything in the name of the Lord); you can look to these things as barometers of how your inner self is growing and being nourished. Some have tried to teach that you'll grow in these things equally at the same pace, but I don't find that lining up with the reality of my life, nor the lives of people who are close to me. Indeed there is growth in all of these; I would even say some of them grow together, like compassion and kindness, humility and patience. Others God seems to grow in their own seasons, like forgiveness and wisdom. The goal, though, is that all of these increase over time in a way that transforms us all into the *same* image of Christ. And this transformation – our sanctification – is a guaranteed work that God promises to finish (Philippians 1:6) in every believer.

Putting on the new self means that we take time to examine our compassion and kindness; to check how well it's growing. We inspect our humility, our patience, our forgiveness, and we take note of our steadfastness. Examination, inspection, both verbs imply that there's a comparison being made. We only need to be careful to make sure we are comparing ourselves to Jesus. Since the Father is transforming us into the likeness of the Son, Jesus is the *only* one we should make *final* comparisons with. How compassionate is Jesus? How humble is Jesus? How patient is Jesus? These are our benchmarks.

I have encountered many people who profess their love for Jesus, but live frustrated spiritual lives. I've been one of them, and frankly I think seasons of spiritual frustration come and go for all of us. If you take time to dig in a little and peel back the surface layers of frustration, many times you will find that you've placed too much faith in the people you look to as models of faith and practice. When you conduct a spiritual inventory on your life, the new self must be compared to the correct manifest.

I am a huge fan of the television series, *Lost*. In case you don't know, the whole show is plotted around the survivors of a plane crash on an uncharted Pacific island. One of the first season plot points is that there are people in the camp of crash survivors who are only pretending to have been on the plane when it crashed. In reality, these men and women are from the island, not the plane, and they have infiltrated the survivor camps as spies for their people. As these spies continue in the camps, they begin abducting survivors, and doing things that frustrate the survivor camps' attempts to get rescued. It isn't until someone finds the passenger manifest that they realize there are people in their number who weren't on the plane. This rings true for our spiritual lives. Until you compare yourself to the manifest – the Word, Jesus the Son – your assessment of yourself will be amiss and you won't be able to determine the cause of your frustrations and failures.

Now, it is true that the Apostle Paul instructed the churches he planted and the people he mentored to imitate him in faith and practice. *Be imitators of me, as I am of Christ* (1 Corinthians 11:1). But he qualifies himself by saying, *as I am of Christ.* The people we imitate in faith and practice must be people who have demonstrated faithfulness to Christ over the long haul. As long as these men and women are faithful in their pursuit of Jesus, you can draw from them as a source of inspiration and model your disciplines after theirs. But remember, *they are a work in progress as well*. Even as they may seem to be wiser than you, more grateful, more at peace, they too are lacking in these areas. They too are looking beyond themselves to measure their spiritual progress. So even as we look to each other for inspiration, for examples of discipline, for encouragement, *we all look beyond each other to Jesus.* He is our ultimate comparison, he is our final authority, he is who we are being fashioned after.

The new self is who you are in Christ. It's who you will be in eternity, it's who you are today. It is the source of your identity. It is the person the Holy Spirit is working diligently to refine and recreate. But the new self is also someone you intentionally put on and nourish daily. The intentionality of the new self is what brings light into the darkness that surrounds you. The new self is constantly examined. Like you would examine a tomato on the vine for ripeness, you examine the new self to ensure that things are progressing toward ripeness. Every season of life is given to ripen aspects of your new self toward spiritual maturity that behaves like, talks like, thinks like Jesus Christ. Seasons of trial grow our patience and endurance. Seasons of peace grow our gratitude and joy. No season is given that won't be used to ripen the new self toward spiritual greatness. Our constant choice is to either regress into a dead life that will only bring death and destruction to everything, or to put on the new self and let every season's purpose ripen and mature us toward Christlikeness.

At the beginning of this chapter I posed a series of questions that are important, and I believe we've begun to answer them here, save one. *How does the new self flourish?* The concept of flourishing goes farther than simply living, it goes beyond remaining healthy enough to endure. I lived on the plains of northeastern Colorado for over a decade, and I've seen this picture repeated many times: a single tree in the middle of miles of empty prairie. This tree grew there because the soil was right, there was a consistent source of water, and the environment was favorable. It turns green in the spring, provides shade in the summer, and sheds it's leaves in the autumn like all healthy trees. This tree is healthy. But is it flourishing?

Flourishing means that you don't just grow and maintain good health, but there's a vigorousness about your growth. A flourishing tree produces fruit that provides seed, that eventually grows more trees. A single lone tree on the prairie may be healthy, but it isn't flourishing. Flourishing is a vigorous existence. It's a multiplying existence. It's an existence where your fullest potential is being realized. Flourishing happens in places where the soil is good for multiplying growth. The new self only flourishes in community within the Body of Christ. Community provides fertile ground to bear fruit and multiply. That's bad news for any professing believer who thinks he or she can isolate and stay clear of people *and* at the same time have a vibrant relationship with God. Let me show you.

The new self has been given spiritual gifts for *serving others*. In multiple places in the New Testament, you find God showing us that each believer is given gifts, according to God's divine purposes. And, those purposes were planned for us in advance.

> Now there are varieties of gifts, but the same Spirit; and there are varieties of service, but the same Lord; and there are varieties of activities, but it is the same God who empowers them all in everyone. To each is given the manifestation of the Spirit for the common good. (1 Corinthians 12:4-7)

> For we are his workmanship, created in Christ Jesus for good works, which God prepared beforehand, that we should walk in them. (Ephesians 2:10)

If you keep reading in 1 Corinthians 12, you'll discover that these spiritual gifts are given so that the Body of Christ – the church – might thrive. For what purpose? Ephesians 2:10 doesn't say exactly what those works are, but it does say that they are works that were prepared beforehand.

Our new selves flourish when we are walking in the works that God prepared beforehand, using the gifts that he gave us to accomplish those works. But the sad reality is that many people talk about living in community and *doing life together*, but so few are actually putting forth the effort that kind of existence requires. And consequently, many believers aren't flourishing. They're enduring. They're surviving. But the kingdom potential they've been given is hardly being tapped. In an interview with Jefferson Bethke, Timothy Keller said this about this generation's desire for community: "The younger generation doesn't want to make the sacrifices that enable community to happen, which means you have to limit your options. You can't just travel everywhere. You can't just move every two years. You can't just live any way you want."[2] To do life together, to be in community with people, means you are committing to *plant* yourself in a place indefinitely to allow time for your life to bear fruit that benefits other people.

All our gifts, all our works, all our purpose is tied up in unity with other believers and mission in the world that's surrounding us. Uprooting yourself from the place where you can have a vigorous existence will reduce you. You'll never be all that God has created you to be if you remain uprooted and unsettled from the community of saints. This is why the author of Hebrews encourages us:

> And let us consider how to stir up one another to love and good works, not neglecting to meet together, as is the habit of some, but encouraging one another, and all the more as you see the Day drawing near. (Hebrews 10:24-25)

Look, I've had times in my life where disconnecting from the church seemed like the most desirable course of action. The Body of Christ is beautiful, but individual believers can be meaner than a junkyard dog. I've experienced church hurt. I've gone through the church hurting other members of my family. I understand the desire to leave and just do Jesus on your own. But friends, that's not how God has designed things. He designed your spiritual life to flourish within the fellowship of the Church. Any other way, and you short yourself. It's the fires of trial that transform us. Put on your new self. Nourish your new self. And plant your new self in the fertile soil of the Church's community where you won't merely endure your time on this broken planet, but you'll flourish with a vigorous existence.

References:
1. The Incredibles. Walt Disney, released 2004.
2. Timothy Keller interview with Jefferson Bethke. https://www.youtube.com/watch?v=ja9U1X3xeSY

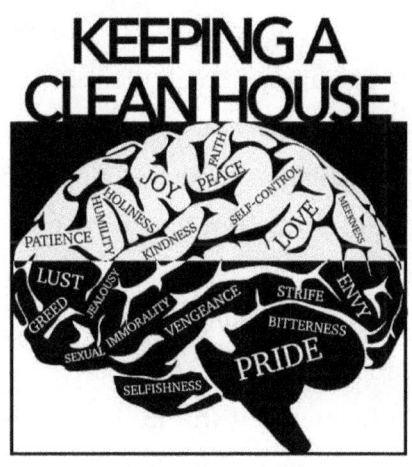

KEEPING A CLEAN HOUSE

Sometime in 2008, Radene and I made the decision to ditch cable television. It's a horrible investment. Think about it: most people complain about the price, and that most of the time there is nothing interesting to watch. If you owned a business and had an employee who was expensive to keep and only occasionally did what you hired him for, you'd fire him. Well, we fired cable television. It made no sense to keep a service that seldom served us the way we wanted. We went from cable television to a little set-top box, hardly known then, but widely known now, called Roku. I'm fairly certain that we were among the earliest adopters of this new wave of streaming technology. From then on, we watched our favorite television shows by streaming it over the Internet through our Roku box.

That move gave us enormous control over what kind of content played on our televisions. Commercials became rare, and with age-appropriate filtering we didn't worry nearly as much about our children accidentally (or purposefully) watching something inappropriate. Those concerns didn't disappear, but they were greatly diminished once we dumped cable television. There's something liberating about asserting control over areas of your life. It really is a paradox. Control and liberty don't seem to be comfortable bedfellows, but truthfully, we are way more at ease when we arrest areas of our lives that seem beyond our control. When we have control over something it ceases to be a source of worry and concern. In fact, God has told us that one of the expressions of the fruit of the Spirit is *self-control* (Galatians 5:22). If you have been born again, the Holy Spirit will manifest in your life through self-control. By the Spirit, believers possess the potential to be the most self-controlled people on the planet. And by that, we would be the most liberated people on the planet as well!

One of the shows that Radene and I have enjoyed streaming together is Hoarders. Perhaps *enjoy* is the wrong word. We watch Hoarders in stunned bewilderment. Those homes defy classification. They're dumps, but everyone calls their home a dump from time to time. Our categories of messy are all defined a little different. These homes utterly destroy your categories for messy. I cannot imagine living in those conditions. I've been to South Africa. I've walked in shanty towns. I've entered the homes of people who live in those shanty towns. I'd rather live there than in the homes on Hoarders. At least the shanty homes I entered were tidy and could be navigated safely.

However, hoarding isn't about being messy, although the result is usually a catastrophic mess of epic proportions. Hoarding is about control. The vast majority of the people showcased on Hoarders are people who have suffered loss or been wounded emotionally and have learned to control their emotions through hoarding. Impulse purchases, insatiable collecting, all the emotional perks that come from finding their treasures insulates them from dealing with their past hurts. The very hoarding that makes them feel good keeps them emotionally unhealthy, and it becomes physically unhealthy in the process. In other words, they're perpetually buying or collecting things to make them feel good in the moment so that they *can't* feel the actual sickness that lies beneath the surface. It's nothing more than a form of control. Control gives us a sense of liberty. As backward as it sounds, hoarders feel liberated from their problems. They do see the mess. They do admit it needs to be cleaned up. But when the cleanup crews show up, they recoil and defend their stuff like a cobra because letting go of their stuff is the same as losing control.

Occasionally, though, we watch an episode of Hoarders that ends extremely well. The home owners are cooperative with the process, even though it's hard for them. There's a kind of reconciliation between the owner and the family they have estranged because of their hoarding. And then the follow-up visit that typically happens a few months after the cleanup reveals that they have maintained a clean home. This never happens because the home owner is some super strong person with rock solid determination to simply grit and grind their way through the aftermath of losing their mountains of stuff. Success like this comes from getting help. They go to counseling. They get help from professional organizers. They get reunited with the loved ones they had pushed away. It indeed does take strength, but it's the kind of strength that is gained from letting people in and becoming vulnerable with those who care about your well-being.

All of us can be spiritual hoarders. I'll go beyond saying that we *can be*; many of us *are presently* spiritual hoarders. Your house is a disaster, cluttered with idols that have either slipped in unnoticed, or have simply been allowed to cohabitate with you and God. And don't think I'm saying this in a vacuum, Jesus said it first. We all have spiritual houses that need to be deep-cleaned. Look at what Jesus says:

> When the unclean spirit has gone out of a person, it passes through waterless places seeking rest, but finds none. Then it says, 'I will return to my house from which I came.' And when it comes, it finds the house empty, swept, and put in order. Then it goes and brings with it seven other spirits more evil than itself, and they enter and dwell there, and the last state of

that person is worse than the first. So also will it be with this evil generation. (Matthew 12:43-45)

There's a few things we can imply from this statement. First is that we all start with a house that needs to be cleansed. When we talked about *out with the old,* the process of cleansing your spiritual house involves getting rid of things that will pull you back into your old way of thinking and living. So when Jesus refers to an unclean spirit that has left a person, this can be a person who has made the initial efforts to rid themselves of the influences, of the idols, and the worldly relationships that would lead them back to their old life. We all start this way in our Christian journey. No one starts with a clean house, so hopefully we all go through this initial cleansing of our lives.

So, you clean your house. You get rid of the bad influences, you stop the bad habits, you remove the junk. Then notice what Jesus says: *when it comes, it finds the house empty, swept, and put in order.* Here's where many people get blind-sided. A clean house doesn't mean it's a godly house. A home can have the appearance of order, where everything has its place, mom and dad love each other, and the children all say *please* and *thank you,* but be devoid of any presence of God. Oh my, have I seen this so many times! Even recently, I've seen people birthed into the kingdom of God, who before I never questioned that they *weren't* Christians because they attended church, they proclaimed a love for Jesus, and were doing their best to live a life that pleases God. You know what that tells me? Satan is satisfied with you living a moral life, *if* it keeps you from being born again. He's okay with you being model church parents, so long as you aren't model Christian parents. You can clean up your life, find fellowship with people of like morals, feel accepted into the community of the Church, and still be spiritually dead on the inside; unsaved, unfilled by the Spirit, yet experiencing something emotionally fulfilling at church that makes you feel a part.

Next, when an unclean spirit comes back to check on his old home, if he sees it's clean, swept, and put in order, he doesn't just move back in, but this time he brings several stronger spirits with him to occupy with greater strength. This implies that whatever it took to force him out the first time, won't cut it next time because now he's seven times stronger with the help of his new roommates. It leads to a very important spiritual principle. A house that gets decluttered and cleaned up is prime real estate for dark spiritual forces to move in and cause havoc. If you *only* clean up your house, but you don't call upon the Lord for salvation, you still have an empty house. Once the Holy Spirit makes your heart his home, a permanent *no vacancy* sign goes up, and no unclean spirit can ever force him out. But until that happens, there is still room in the inn. This is why Jesus said the last state of this person is worse than the first. A person purged of one unclean spirit, but never filled by the Holy Spirit, will only end up reoccupied by more unclean spirits than he or she had to begin with.

So, let me stop here and clarify something. These verses we're examining have a very direct application for unbelieving people. Jesus is warning the religious leaders of his day, who were rejecting him, that their disbelief toward him was only strengthening the demonic forces at work behind their rejection. And if they continued to place their faith in the morality of the Law, as perfect as the Law is, but reject the Holy Spirit's work in Jesus' ministry, they would find themselves bound up in their disbelief by even stronger demonic powers. That's exactly what happens to so many unsaved church folks. They have trusted a belief in morality, a belief in an experience, a belief in what their parents raised them to believe, but they've never actually been born again. That's demonic, inasmuch as it blinds you to your real spiritual condition. And it's no different than what was happening with the Pharisees and Scribes. They too were blinded by their beliefs, their morality, and their traditions which made them feel like they were spiritual people, despite being spiritually dead.

But these verses also have application to believers. While what Jesus is saying here speaks of unclean spirits that are occupying people, which is something that cannot happen to people who've been born again (a demon cannot inhabit a person once the Holy Spirit has taken residence), to say that believers are impervious to demonic activity is incorrect. In light of this, let's examine the importance for every believer to keep a clean house. You can look in many Christian homes today and find a plaque that reads those famous words from

Joshua 24:15b, *"But as for me and my house, we will serve the Lord."* It's one thing to make that declaration for your home, it's something else entirely to live by that declaration and walk in the fullness of what it meant when Joshua said it.

What seldom gets quoted with Joshua's declaration is the preceding parts of his statement. *"And if it is evil in your eyes to serve the Lord, choose this day whom you will serve, whether the gods your fathers served in the region beyond the River, or the gods of the Amorites in whose land you dwell."* (Joshua 24:15a). Deciding to serve the Lord is not only an embrace of Jesus Christ, but a rejection of all other gods that you have allowed to dominate your life. You can't embrace Jesus, and keep your gods. You can't welcome the Holy Spirit into your life and continue to give room and board to unclean spirits. Embracing Jesus *is* rejecting every other lower-case savior.

Inevitably, when the unclean spirit keeps coming up empty handed on finding a new home, he decides to return to his old home – you – to see what's happening. He can't enter like he once did because you have a new resident – the Holy Spirit. So unclean spirits do the next best thing: they set out baits to lure you outside, away from the safe fellowship you have within with the Spirit of God. If you go out, you become vulnerable. If you fall for the lures, you'll be wide open to attack. Do you have a sin that keeps entangling you? Do you have destructive forces in your life that threaten you on repeat? Spiritually speaking, the unclean spirits that once found a home in your life, are always coming back by to see what you've done with the place since they were evicted.

And if you aren't in order, you'll fall for their tricks to pull you away from your relationship with God.

On any given episode of National Geographic, much to my wife's dismay, you might see a lion chase down and eat an antelope. You may witness a zebra get devoured by a cheetah. While many times the victims are the weak and sick, sometimes you have an antelope that gets separated from the herd. Something got its attention, a smell, a sound, and it wanders away from the safety of the larger group. Then a lioness catches a glimpse of this stray antelope. Her head dips, her body crouches close to the ground, she hides herself in the tall grasses of the savannah, and she creeps. The longer the antelope is captivated away from the herd, the more opportunity multiplies for the lioness. She creeps, close, and then she pounces, and the chase is on! (Queue the National Geographic music!) Sometimes it ends well for the antelope, other times it ends well for the lioness! This is exactly how it is for us when we leave the safety of fellowship with the Holy Spirit. Sometimes we realize that we've gone out of bounds before it costs us too much. Other times we get entangled and trapped, giving our enemies an open season for attack.

What does it mean to keep a clean house? It means remaining in fellowship with the Holy Spirit and letting him keep things in order. The moment we start trying arrange the furniture, the moment we stop listening to the Spirit of God and start listening to the sounds beyond of the safety of the house, we enter into a place of insecurity and unrest. How then do we train ourselves in the practice of remaining in safe fellowship with God's Spirit? Let me highlight a few foundational things that shape your spiritual house. For every believer, there are issues of the heart, the mind, and spirit that frame our relationship with the Holy Spirit. He knows us perfectly, so the learning curve is on our end. The impetus is upon us to learn of Him in the way the He knows us.

The nature and quality of the spiritual house of all believers is that of freedom. Take in the following:

> So if the Son sets you free, you will be free indeed. (John 8:36)
>
> For freedom Christ has set us free; stand firm therefore, and do not submit again to a yoke of slavery. (Galatians 5:1)
>
> Now the Lord is the Spirit, and where the Spirit of the Lord is, there is freedom. (2 Corinthians 3:17)
>
> Live as people who are free, not using your freedom as a cover-up for evil, but living as servants of God. (1 Peter 2:16)

Salvation brings freedom. Being in Christ is the greatest liberty you will experience on this earth. It's greater than any liberty that government can offer. It's better than any freedom you can experience from *doing it your way*. And, as a believer, your experience of this liberty is totally dependent on the health and status of your relationship with the Holy Spirit. There is a holy work that each of us must do so that we can experience our liberty in Christ to the fullest. This is where a paradox comes into play.

Our understanding of freedom is tainted by how the world defines freedom. The picture of freedom that many of us Americans have is one of self-determination. We are the makers of our own destinies, and the less the government interferes with rules and regulations, the better off we will be. We've allowed that understanding of freedom to influence our understanding of Christian liberty. So as we discuss the foundational things that shape our spiritual house, we'll discover that there are disciplines, there are commands, there are things that we *must* obey so that our relationship with the Holy Spirit will thrive. These will lead us to the liberty promised for every believer.

First, there are issues of the heart that we must tend. A while back, I had a conversation with my daughter, Phoebe. She was about to embark on her first big trip away from home without her parents. Mom and I weren't going with her for those next three days. She was going to be in Nashville and we would be in Salem, six hours away. While driving her to school, I told her that a clean conscience is one of the most liberating things we can have, and to do things that require lying and secret keeping will only make her life more complicated. I said other things, but my point to her was that while she's away she should make decisions that would do

Jesus proud, do us proud, and do her school proud. If Phoebe conducts herself in a way that won't require deception when she returns home, she'll have no reason to fear, and therefore she'll walk in liberty. Even if she makes a bad decision while in Nashville, upon returning home being immediately honest with me will incur less discipline than me finding out from someone else later. There's always more liberty with integrity and confession than with keeping secrets and covering up your actions with falsehoods.

Integrity and confession are issues that spring from the heart. The new heart we receive when we're born again is a gift from God. Integrity is something that God desires for us and is something he has planted within our new heart's desires. Proverbs 11:3 says, *"The integrity of the upright guides them, but the crookedness of the treacherous destroys them."* To be a person of integrity simply means that you conduct your life in a way that you have nothing to be ashamed of before God. You live your whole life, publicly and privately, as before the Lord. Therefore, you are the same person in public as you are in private. This sounds so simple, but it is in this area where many believers find themselves lacking. It is this area that creates all sorts of disarray in our spiritual houses. Why do so many find it difficult to be people of integrity before the Lord?

Our difficulty with integrity boils down to a simple truth: we don't fully believe that Jesus is better. We believe that he saves, we believe that he delivers us from death and the grave, we believe he gives us access to the Father, we believe that eternal life is found in Christ, but we don't believe that our greatest experience of life on this earth is *also* found in Christ. What do I mean? Maybe the clearest example I can give you is the issue of sex. An article on Christianpost.com from February 12, 2014 cites a survey conducted by Christian Mingle which reported that only eleven percent of the professing Christians surveyed were waiting until marriage to have sex.[1] I think the writing on the wall is clear. We trust him for eternal life, but we don't trust him for abundant life here on earth. This is a huge issue of belief! The mind that isn't fully convinced of the abundant life that Christ promises while we're still in this life will be at odds with the Holy Spirit residing within. You show me a believer who wrestles with integrity, and I'll show you a believer who doesn't trust all the promises of abundant life that come through Jesus. Until you believe that all the promises of God find their *yes* in Christ (2 Corinthians 1:20), you will put your trust elsewhere when it comes to finding a fuller satisfaction in this life.

However, it's not all bad news. The truth is because we're still trapped in this rotting, decaying, unredeemed flesh, all believers will stumble in their integrity; all believers will wrestle to believe the promises of God for us in this life. The good news is even when we walk with imperfect integrity, we can still keep a clean spiritual home and remain in intimate fellowship with the Holy Spirit if we are faithful to confess. Confession is also an issue of the heart. Our new hearts will naturally desire to love God and do what pleases him. In fact you could say that a life of integrity is also a life filled with confession. When we stop confessing that's when we believe that we're okay on our own and our integrity slips. So what does it mean to confess?

Confession is something that all believers are to make a part of their spiritual disciplines. James 5:16 instructs us to *confess our sins to one another, that you may be healed.* This healing goes far beyond the physical. There's also a spiritual healing that happens when we confess our sins. And notice it says *to one another*, not to a preacher. You don't have to find a pastor to do confession. All you need is a fellow believer whom you trust and will provide accountability for you. This confession of sin is an acknowledgment that you've sinned against God, and if genuine, a resolve to cease sinning. When we confess to one another, we admit before God and our brothers that we have been wrong and that we desire to restore right fellowship. This itself is an act of integrity because it brings out into the light the things that you could've kept in the shadows (although nothing is in the shadows for God).

There's nothing quite so liberating as confession of sin. It allows you to keep walking in integrity. I've had many moments of confession where a burden was lifted and I could physically feel the difference within me. My heart experienced healing, my countenance was lifted, my perspective shifted, and even the thought of suffering the consequences of telling the truth felt righteous and desirable. A long time ago, I offended a friend of mine. She and I had served together on our church's worship team and had a healthy friendship. A series of events happened, and I ended up becoming the worship leader in our church. To be brief, I made some leadership mistakes that ultimately hurt my friend, and caused a rift in our friendship. In fact, after that you could scarcely consider us friends. I was too proud to admit my mistake, she was too hurt to continue the friendship, so for a while, things were radio silent.

During that time, I felt the awkwardness. I cringed at encountering her in public. When I did see her, my heart sank. Eventually, God force fed me some perspective. I first went to where her husband worked, and I apologized to him. Why? Because I hurt his wife. He had some things to say, but I remained silent. It wasn't loud, or ugly; it just was. Then after a while, I apologized to her. After that day, my heart shifted. I was no longer uneasy about seeing her in public. The awkwardness lifted. I felt physically different. I wish I could tell you everything was restored to better than before, but I can tell you that I did as much as I could to restore peace and confess my sin. In confessing, my integrity was restored, the Holy Spirit was no longer grieved over my ongoing sin (as long as I wasn't apologizing, I was disobeying the Spirit), and I found deeper fellowship with the Lord. Integrity and confession are core issues of the heart that must be tended and kept if we're going to keep a clean spiritual house where the Holy Spirit is given full reign.

Then there are issues of the mind. In chapter one, I laid out the Biblical emphasis on renewing your mind. I don't want to restate all of that again, but instead let me share with you some disciplines that have been helpful to me. First, and probably foremost, remember that your thoughts *are not private*. When you were born again, your heart became the home, the Temple, the dwelling place of the Holy Spirit. Think of it this way. He's at home in your heart, sitting on the couch, watching all your thoughts on a huge 3D, ultra-high definition screen. Nothing slips by, no thought escapes the broadcast. So whatever you're thinking, the Holy Spirit, third member of the Godhead, the seal of your redemption is getting a front row private viewing. You take him in the gutter, you take him through the day dream. He sees your brainstorming, and he sees your scheming. Nothing is hidden from him. If your relationship with him means anything to you, this should give you huge cause for pause before you let your mind drift any way the wind blows.

Second, and very practically, stop flooding your mind with things that displease the Lord. Because we are still living in this world, you can't escape one hundred percent of the garbage out there, but that's not really what I'm talking about. Many of us *flood* our minds with worldly stuff very intentionally (movies, television, music, media, images, etc.), and then wonder why we can't seem to live in victory over our besetting sins. I'll tell you from experience with pornography, that it doesn't take much to trigger the journey down the path to indulging. I could see an image of a scantly clad woman, or read something that wasn't pornographic per say, but was certainly evocative, and that would be the first domino to fall. Mind you, the dangerous thing about this is those triggers didn't necessarily always work. So, one day a Sports Illustrated swimsuit model may not trigger anything, but the next, it might.

Eventually, the light bulb came on: just don't risk it at all. Since that moment, I have been intentional to *not* view video or images or read articles that might be a trigger. That changed my entertainment choices. I read IMDB's parent guide about almost every movie I watch before I watch it. If it lists nudity or strong sexual content, I won't watch. If a PG-13 movie is too blatantly sexual, I won't watch it. I don't watch unrated movies. I no longer listen to music that objectifies women (believe it or not, when I was much younger, I listened almost exclusively to hip hop). I no longer intentionally expose my mind to entertainment that could trigger my lust. Is the entertainment to blame? No, the blame would lie upon me for consuming it, but I would be foolish to entrap myself. Am I suggesting everyone take on my approach? Not necessarily. Some of you may need something even more restrictive, but I'll be direct with you. If you can make any justification for anyone who professes Christ to watch any movie or television with blatant nudity and sex, then you must not be reading the same Bible as me. Do what you can to *not* flood your mind. Enough will happen that's beyond your control; you shouldn't pile garbage upon garbage.

Third, declare the truth to yourself. I've heard it said many times that every day we should preach the gospel to ourselves. That doesn't mean you need to hear a sermon every day. Nor does that mean you need to read about the crucifixion every day. What it does mean is that every day needs to contain a reminder that you don't deserve the grace you've received in Christ. 2 Corinthians 5:21 is a great verse to include in your daily reminders. In this single verse, you have the essential truths of the whole gospel captured.

> For our sake he made him to be sin who knew no sin, so that in him we might become the righteousness of God.

For our sake. The reason Jesus went to the cross was for *our sake*. The plan that God has for salvation was put into motion in eternity past for the sole purpose of redeeming a people for himself, with whom he can personally dwell for the rest of eternity. Don't get the wrong idea. God wasn't lonely. He was perfectly content in eternity between Father, Son, and Spirit before he created us. But just like any artist doesn't find the fullest joy in his work until it is shared with the world, God couldn't help but create a people with whom he would share himself. And *for our sake*, he has offered salvation through Jesus, so that we can enter the eternal joys of residing with him.

He made him to be sin who knew no sin. The plan was for Jesus, the one who knew no sin, to come and take our sins upon himself. It was a substitution, *for our sake*. We deserved the penalty of death for our sins, but Jesus came and undeservingly died the death that we most definitely deserved. If Jesus has taken your sins, you are no longer indebted to sin's penalty. You are debt free because Jesus paid your debt, *for your sake*.

So that in him we might become the righteousness of God. His substitution on our behalf makes possible for us to be declared righteous, but not it's not a righteousness that we earn; it's God's righteousness that covers us. None of this was anything we could do. It was God's plan to redeem us, it was God's plan to substitute for us, it was his plan to give us his own righteousness. We are undeserving benefactors of divine grace. Nothing we do makes us deserve it, and nothing we do causes us to lose it. We are simply debtors to God's grace, and *that* is where the transforming power of the gospel lies.

That is what we need to remember every day. I need to look in the mirror and remind myself daily that because of Christ, *I am presently* the righteousness of God. So do you. If I am *presently* the righteousness of God, then I am presently empowered with everything I need to live a life that pleases him. And since Jesus *substituted* for us, taking our penalty *for our sake*, then the gratitude and love that flows from knowing this is what fuels and propels us forward in our spiritual growth. Why would anyone want to displease someone who sacrificed so much for our sake? Walking out into the world each day with a fresh reminder of the grace we've received helps keep our affections for Jesus greater than our affections for our sin.

Finally, there are issues of the spirit. It's hard to talk about the spirit independent from the heart and the mind because they're all connected, three parts of a whole. But there are issues that affect the spirit which will defy the desires of your heart, and confound how you've equipped your mind. If the heart is the center of your desires, and the mind is the center of planning and action, the spirit is the source of your countenance. It's more than your mood and emotions, it's the temperament of your entire personality. Your spirit is the essence of who you are in Christ. It's your person. It's the person the Holy Spirit is shaping and molding into the likeness of Jesus. And it can be affected separately from the heart and the mind. Take this for example.

Have you ever been in a place in life, where your heart desires to pursue the Lord, your mind knows what you need to do, but you simply lack any motivation to do what it takes? That's a spiritual problem. Maybe you've been discouraged. Perhaps you've been let down by people one too many times. Whatever it may be, it has drained your motivation to actually pursue the Lord, and so you remain in a stagnate spiritual condition. I think many of us have been here multiple times in our spiritual lives. Sometimes we are depressed. Other times we allow anger to have control and bitterness sets in. And despite what we know is right in our hearts and minds, we are unable or unwilling to pursue Jesus like we should because our spirits are troubled.

How can we keep a clean spiritual house, when our spirits are embattled with their own issues? This is always,

always, always an issue of obeying the Holy Spirit, but it cuts deeper and broader than you might imagine. God doesn't only want your spirit, he wants your entire life; physical and spiritual. Don't you see that the physical has a direct impact on the spiritual? If you don't give the Holy Spirit control of the physical aspects of your life, your spiritual self is going to be malnourished and wounded.

I'm not sure that I've heard a better explanation of this concept than from Timothy Keller. On December 5, 2004, he preached a sermon called *The Wounded Spirit*. He dives into the topic of spiritual health, and how to heal a wounded, crushed spirit. The inner life of your spirit is the most important thing in your life. Proverbs 18:14 says, *"A man's spirit will endure sickness, but a crushed spirit who can bear?"* In other words, your spirit is what sustains you through sickness and hardship, but if you have a crushed spirit, you have a diminished capacity for enduring anything! I can't deal with all the depth he brings in his entire sermon, but he makes a statement in the midst that I think captures what I'm trying to tell you here. He says:

> Unless you're living with every aspect of your being before God, you are going to have despondency. You are going to have out-of-control emotions. You're going to have despair. You're going to have a crushed spirit you will not be able to remedy. You'll get the books, and you'll go and listen to people who tell you

the way to emotional health. They'll always be too simple. They'll always be foolish.[2]

Keeping a clean spiritual house means giving the Holy Spirit rule over every area of your life, over all your appetites. Food. Sex. Drink. Wealth. Relationships. Whatever else you crave in the physical world, the Spirit is asking for control over those things. Do you realize that sometimes you are depressed (I don't mean necessarily in the clinical sense) because you over indulged in certain kinds of food for too long? Too much unhealthy, unbalanced eating affects your chemistry and swings your mood. You get irritable, your mind is unable to think as clearly, your judgment becomes impaired. I'm not making this up, it's documented and researched. Too much sugar impairs your thinking. It puts you in a constant dopamine high[3], which is the same thing that cocaine does[4]. And when the sugar flow stops, you have a dopamine crash, which leads to a change in mood, perhaps even symptoms of depression... all from over indulging sugar.

If we give the Holy Spirit control of our appetites for food, he's going to lead us into moderation. He's going to keep us from over-indulging. He's going to help us remain sober-minded. A Spirit-controlled diet keeps us from the spiritual damage that comes from a lack of self-control in our appetite for food. This applies across the appetite spectrum, from food to sex to everything else. Giving him control over them will protect our spirits and keep us in a healthy place physically, emotionally, relationally, and spiritually. If you are sober-minded, if you have allowed God to have control of your appetites, then you will have the clarity you need to recognize when those unclean spirits are trying to lure you away from the peace and safety of your spiritual home with the Spirit of God.

This is ongoing. This is the constant work of every believer who pursues intimacy with the Father. It's the part of our faith journey that's at the same time the most frustrating, and the most grace bearing. We *will* fail at this, and God's grace *will* catch us. We *will* stray from the light, and the grace of God *will* bring us back into the light. It isn't how badly we beat ourselves up, or how much correction we receive that transforms us when we fail. Transformation comes from the embrace of grace that says, *let's begin again*. Every new start in this journey begins with the grace that caught us after our failure. A clean spiritual house is mopped with God's grace as we allow the Holy Spirit to lead us in all things. Don't be discouraged by failure. God certainly isn't. He knows the work he's doing in us will be completed. We're the ones that get all bent out of shape, not him. Keep calm, and trust him.

References:
1. http://www.christianpost.com/news/christian-dating-culture-part-1-majority-of-single-christians-reject-idea-of-waiting-for-marriage-to-have-sex-114422/
2. http://www.gospelinlife.com/the-wounded-spirit-5399
3. http://www.medicaldaily.com/dopamine-surge-may-explain-your-overeating-insulin-shown-activate-reward-signals-your-359222
4. https://www.drugabuse.gov/publications/research-reports/cocaine/how-does-cocaine-produce-its-effects

Way back in 1997, probably one of the most popular songs of the year was really catchy. I still get its lyrics stuck in my head. The band was Chumbawamba. The song was *Tubthumping,* a.k.a. *I Get Knocked Down.* The chorus lyric goes:

>I get knocked down, but I get up again
>You are never gonna keep me down
>I get knocked down, but I get up again
>You are never gonna keep me down
>I get knocked down, but I get up again
>You are never gonna keep me down
>I get knocked down, but I get up again
>You are never gonna keep me down [1]

So this guy can't seem to stand up for very long. And it's because he drinks a whiskey drink, then a vodka drink, then a lager drink, then a cider drink. Then he falls down, gets up again, and then he starts over. What a guy! What stamina! This guy has some real staying power. And I hate this song with furious passion because it always gets stuck in my head. Even now, I'll have to hope this song gets purged from my mind quickly! But I bring it up because as ridiculous as the song is, it well portrays the idea that I'm heading for.

One of the simplest lessons a parent teaches their children is to get back up. They fall down, we tell them to get back up. Shake the dust off, and keep playing. There are some parents who try to keep their kids from ever falling by hovering and watching their every move, but honestly that is a fool's errand. Falling will happen now, or it'll happen later. And the older they get, the likelier it'll hurt worse. But the point I'm moving toward is not about the falling; it's about the getting back up. It's the work of keeping up the effort. When we're young, this effort comes a little easier. But as we age, as the world takes its sucker punches, as people disappoint us, we may find the motivation to keep getting back up waning.

And not only do the ebbs and flows of life slowly drain our motivation to get back up, but in a culture that has adopted the motto, *you only live once*, (which is a lie) there is an underlying pressure to live it up, have fun, and enjoy life. Of course, there's nothing wrong with enjoying life, but the insidious side effect is that we devalue things that require struggle. If we only live once, then we don't have time for things that are painful. We don't have time for things that require personal sacrifice. We don't have time for things that don't have a quick return on emotional investment. We expect a fast dividend, an immediate perk, a near instant reciprocation of our efforts. And if that doesn't happen, many people declare, *whatever*, and move on to someone or something that will satisfy their expectations on their terms. There's no desire to struggle, there's few thoughts of waiting, there's little patience for cultivation, the primary impulse is to move on and find something or someone *better*.

This has eroded our endurance. As a people, we generally have very low stamina for struggle. I want to be careful here because this doesn't apply *carte blanche* to everyone. There are some among us who have endured many difficult struggles, and I respect that. But there are many in our midst who fold very quickly when the pressure begins to rise. Let me give you a few broad stroke examples. There are serial relationship people. One after the other, there's a path of abandoned relationships in the rearview mirror; there's no lasting commitment. Another is the serial job switcher. If your resume is constantly a year here, six months there, but no real lengthy employment with anyone, you probably either jump ship when things aren't to your liking, or you're very unreliable. In either case, that makes you a bad employee. One more: the serial victim. This person is never at fault when things go south. There's a continuous string of events where this person claims victim status. Rather than take responsibility for mistakes, the serial victim never claims responsibility, never wants to be perceived as the bad guy, never wants to be the cause of something that went wrong because victims are always pitied and always let off the hook.

Now, as I said, those were broad strokes. They don't consider extenuating circumstances, they don't consider the exceptions to the rule, they're broad swipes with a huge brush. Being broad strokes, though, means that they probably hit a few people right between the eyes, and hit most people as a glancing blow. It may not completely describe you, but it does a little bit in a few situations. So nearly everyone is affected by this in some way, even if only a little. And if you're one of the few to whom this doesn't apply, you for sure know someone affected. As a nation, we have a severely diminished stamina for hardship. We have a very low endurance for struggle. And I submit to you this stems from a spiritual problem. We possess no spiritual stamina at all, or low spiritual stamina.

Of course, when I say spiritual stamina, that implies there's a spirit alive within you trying to make a way. Biblically, you can only have spiritual stamina, even if it's low, if you are born again. Before the Holy Spirit gives us new birth, we are spiritually dead, and dead people have zero stamina. The Bible explains our dead condition prior to being born again.

> And you were *dead* in the trespasses and sins in which you once walked, following the course of this world,

following the prince of the power of the air, the spirit that is now at work in the sons of disobedience (Ephesians 2:1-2)

Therefore, to possess spiritual stamina at all means you must be born again into the kingdom of God. What does it look like? Have you ever seen the Steve McQueen movie, *Papillon*? Based on a true story, McQueen's character is wrongfully imprisoned for life in French Guiana for a murder he didn't commit. The entire movie is about his numerous escapes from prison over the course of his life. At one point in the movie, after being recaptured, he's sentenced to solitary. The cells were built into the ground with an open ceiling, covered by bars, which had a catwalk on top where the guards could patrol. In solitary, there was no talking, but there's this one scene where McQueen waits for the guard to pass, and he jumps, grabs the bars, pulls himself up, and defiantly whispers, "I'm still here!"

That's the kind of spiritual stamina I want to have! When I get knocked down, I want to get up, collect myself, and defiantly declare to my enemies, *I'm still here!* Christ within me is greater than any power outside of me, and because of him I'm still here! I want to have that kind of stick-it-to-my-enemy attitude. At times, I have to say it to myself because often I'm my own worst enemy.

So the question at hand is how do you increase your spiritual stamina? How do we go from having low stamina to high stamina spiritually speaking? We've covered so much in this book, from choices, to new disciplines, to discerning spirits, to keeping a clean spiritual house, but the issue that we encounter on repeat is that we are never finished. We're perpetually in need of wisdom, godly choices, discernment, and a clean spiritual home. There's never a time where we can survey the landscape of our life and declare a holiday from the grind. So the choice is really one of two: you can either develop spiritual stamina, or you can become spiritually ineffective.

Perhaps the best bad example I can think of in the Scripture is King David. I know that we like to paint David as this example of a godly king who is also a giant slayer, warrior, poet, and all around likeable guy, but David was flawed just like us. David had multiple wives and he was a poor father to his children. For all of the success God granted him on the battlefield, he struggled to remain godly on the home front. Unfortunately, his success as king overshadowed his failures as a husband and father. Perhaps he had become so accustomed to winning, that he thought for sure his household would be in good order. But the truth is, David had it backwards. What happens in your private life always finds its way into your public life. If you're irresponsible at home, you'll eventually become irresponsible at work. If you're angry with your spouse and kids, with the right pressures, you'll lash out in public. David thought that his success as king would bleed into his home and make him a successful husband and father, but the opposite happened. His lack of stamina at home crept into his role as king.

Where this finally caught up to him was in the spring. If you trace out the passage of time in 2 Samuel, this particular spring happens about ten years into David's rule over all of Israel, and about seventeen years after he was crowned king at Hebron (2 Samuel 5:4-5). By this time, David had already married seven women, and bore children with six of them. David also had concubines, but the Bible is unclear as to how many. David may have been an awesome warrior and king, but he couldn't keep his pants on. He refused to be faithful to one wife. And the fact that he had concubines means that he couldn't remain faithful to seven wives either. David was a terrible husband. By the time we arrive at this fateful spring, David had been married to his first wife, Michal, for about twenty-five years. He had added six more wives along the way. You can argue that Michal was barren, so he married again to bear children, which was a custom in ancient times, but that doesn't adequately explain everything. David's second wife, Ahinoam bore him children, yet he continued to marry more women and get concubines.

David's private life was a mess. The man we saw fleeing from King Saul, and trusting the Lord for his life in 1 Samuel experienced a change along the way. His private devotion waned. It's almost as if the moment he finally became king, his private life began to slip and his commitment to personal holiness began to fade. He sought the Lord for big kingly duties like battles, and leadership decisions, but he became comfortable with his own wisdom at home. Soon after, he lacked any spiritual stamina to remain faithful to the Lord's decrees about multiple wives (Deuteronomy 17:17). Then, what he lacked in private made its appearance during the spring of his seventeenth year as king.

> In the spring of the year, the time when kings go out to battle, David sent Joab, and his servants with him, and all Israel. And they ravaged the Ammonites and besieged Rabbah. But David remained at Jerusalem. (2 Samuel 11:1)

David shirked his responsibility to go out to war. His lack of spiritual stamina in private had finally made its debut in his kingly responsibilities. And what happens next is a fateful decision that ripples through the rest of David's life.

> It happened, late one afternoon, when David arose from his couch and was walking on the roof of the king's house, that he saw from the roof a woman bathing; and the woman was very beautiful. And David sent and inquired about the woman. And one said, "Is not this Bathsheba, the daughter of Eliam, the wife of Uriah the Hittite?" So David sent messengers and took her, and she came to him, and he lay with her. (Now she had been purifying herself from her uncleanness.) Then she returned to her house. And the woman conceived, and she sent and told David, "I am pregnant." (2 Samuel 11:2-5)

Allow me to condense the rest of this story for you. David attempts to cover things up. He brings Uriah home from battle, gets him drunk, tries to send him home to his wife, where he would hopefully make love to her, and then the pregnancy could be attributed to him. But Uriah was an honorable man, and refused to have relations with his wife while his friends were still at war, unable to enjoy their wives. Uriah stayed at the palace instead of going home. So David reasoned that the only way to make this sinful pregnancy legitimate was to have Uriah killed, and to marry Bathsheba. And this he did. And the cover up lasted until shortly after the baby was born, when Nathan, the prophet, confronted David about his sin.

What you see for the rest of David's life is the consequences of his sins in private coming home to roost. First, the baby fell ill and died. Then his sons and daughter from his wives start acting a fool, raping, and killing each other. One of his sons, Absalom, led a coup and drove David out of Jerusalem for a short time, but then he was killed when David's army retook the city. His son, Solomon, whom he bore with Bathsheba, continued the family tradition of polygamy, but only upped the ante. David had eight wives, but Solomon amassed seven hundred wives. Consequently, shortly after his death, the kingdom divided because Solomon, for all his wisdom, failed to raise a son who loved the Lord and sought his leadership to rule.

I know that's all very condensed, but it boils down the essence of David's failure. His lack of spiritual stamina didn't just affect him. It affected generations. Because he let his private devotion wane, his private life at home withered on the vine. And his children carried on the seeming lack of concern for spiritual matters at home that they witnessed in their father. And please hear me: I'm not pointing out David's failure to reduce him, but only to point out that like all of us, he had struggles. David's struggles to be a godly husband and parent should resonate with all of us. It should serve as a warning to us to remain vigilant in our devotion to Jesus. But I fear that too often we see the struggles of the godly giants of our faith, and we take that as permission to be *okay* with our struggles, rather than an admonition to avoid them. Knowing that our forefathers in the faith wrestled with sin should comfort us that it is normal to struggle, but it should never make us *okay* with our sin. Sin is never *okay*. It's normal, but it should never become something we're *okay* with.

So how do we grow in spiritual stamina? The first step is the same for everyone, and it's the same as increasing your physical stamina. You must acknowledge that you're not okay. I've been overweight most of my adult life, and for a lot of my childhood. I've only experienced a few precious years where you could say I was a healthy weight. But, because most of my life has been spent overweight, I haven't really given much thought to how unhealthy I could get. I'm used to the man in the mirror. I'm comfortable in my own skin. I have a beautiful wife who has told me time and time again that she loves me and accepts me how I am, period. I have a core of wonderful friends who have never once judged me over my waistline. Everything in my life tells me I'm okay, except the numbers. The numbers I see on the scale not only tell me I'm not okay, but they tell me that eventually things *will* become way worse. So for the last three or four years, I have been on an up and down journey to rectify this situation. I've had to acknowledge the problem and work to change it. And it has been hard! There have been times I've wanted to quit. Honestly, I have quit a few times, but I've always come back because the numbers don't lie. If I don't lose weight, I will develop conditions that will threaten my life. I'm not okay and I'm trying to do something about it.

Spiritually speaking, it's the same. You're okay, in the sense that you're saved and forgiven, but you're *not* okay in the sense that apart from the Vine, you can do nothing. We get comfortable with the nominal conditions of our churches. Everyone sins. Everyone struggles with prayer. Everyone, everyone, everyone… and that lulls us to sleep. Instead of seeing the struggles of others, and letting them serve as a warning, we use them to justify our own struggles. *We're all sinners saved by grace.* [sigh…] While that statement is absolutely true, it is often abused as a justification for being okay with our sins instead of an expression of gratitude for the unmerited grace we've received. If you want your life to count for something in the Kingdom, if you want to make a difference for your King, you will need to be utterly dependent on a thriving relationship with the Holy Spirit within you. That takes an investment of time. It takes a commitment to keep getting up after failures. It requires an acknowledgment that your *absolutely not* okay with the sin in your life because it grieves the Holy Spirit! Spiritual stamina starts with the determination to deal with your sins, not merely learn how to coexist with them. The Apostle John penned it first:

> *If we say we have no sin, we deceive ourselves, and the truth is not in us.* If we confess our sins, he is faithful and just to forgive us our sins and to cleanse us from all unrighteousness. *If we say we have not sinned, we make him a liar, and his word is not in us.* (1 John 1:8-10)

One way I was able to be okay with my obesity for so long is because I never stepped on the scale. I knew I was overweight; the mirror told me so. My frayed belt holes were telling me so. The numerous jeans that were a casualty to my expanding hind parts were telling me so. But I kept sucking in, and using that same belt hole, and putting on those worn out jeans, and avoiding the scale. I kept telling myself it's not as bad as it seems, besides, I still feel good, I still have my strength, I'm good. As long as those cold, harsh numbers never crossed my vision, I could pretend that I was big-boned and healthy.

If we say we have no sin, we deceive ourselves, and the truth is not in us. I've never heard anyone claim they're sinless. No

Christian in their right mind should ever make that claim. Every believer admits that they still sin. But just like I was deceiving myself by never stepping on the scale to allow the gravity (literally) of my situation sink in, when we aren't faithfully exposing ourselves to the truth, reading and meditating on the Word, *we deceive ourselves*, and literally, *the truth is not in us*. That doesn't necessarily mean we're not born again, but it definitely means that the Word of God has not been planted in our minds to keep us aware of our situation. Whenever we step out of the Word of God and neglect to make regular deposits of truth into our minds, we slowly forget. We forget that our sin is crouching, waiting for its next chance to have us. We forget that we are no match for the powers of sin and Satan. We forget that this world is always working to seduce us into conformity. We forget that we need daily fillings of power from the Holy Spirit to bring the Kingdom of God wherever we go. We're all easily forgetful and easily deceived when it comes to spiritual matters. We can't afford to step away from the Word.

At our church, the sound booth is in the balcony. It wasn't my design choice, it was made before I arrived here. If I could move it, I would, but it would require ripping apart a whole bunch of stuff. We'll make do. Being the worship pastor, I make regular trips to the sound booth during the week as I prepare for each of our worship gatherings. That means a lot of stair climbing. One day, I don't remember exactly when, I got to the top of the stairs and it was suddenly very apparent to me that I was breathing heavy and perspiring lightly. I sat down in the booth, tried to do what I came there for, but I couldn't catch my breath. It was a strange feeling. I had never felt it like this. I had been winded before, but not like this. This was my body firing a warning shot across the bow. *Hey, fatty, you can't even climb stairs anymore.* That next morning I stepped on the scale, and I had tipped three hundred pounds. My heart sunk. What had I done? My physical stamina was evaporating. My mind was inundated by thoughts of needing to ride a motorized cart in Walmart because I wouldn't have the physical stamina to walk around the store. That was it for me. I began my rocky, up and down journey to better health. I got a jogging partner, someone thinner, but just as easily winded as me, and we started jogging. I started weighing myself regularly, exposing myself to the truth sometimes every day, but for sure multiple times a week.

Guess what? I've discovered over the past few years of this health journey that the only time I do well is when I am getting regular reminders of the truth. I know this because sometimes I wane from regular weighing, and eventually my weight begins to rise again. In 2016 I lost almost forty pounds. That was the most progress I had made at one swoop since I began this journey a few years ago. But somewhere in the middle of summer, I stopped weighing. We went to a barbeque, I over indulged a bit, and the next morning I didn't weigh because I knew what it was going to show. It was going to remind me of what I did the day before. Not wanting to feel the full force of the guilt, I refrained from weighing.

And again the next day. Gradually, especially once autumn came and the temperatures dropped, I exercised less. I have a treadmill, but that even fell to the wayside. I got comfortable again. I wasn't weighing, I wasn't exercising, and I wasn't strict on my food intake. I knew I was undisciplined, but I told myself I'd get back to it. By the time I got back to it, it was spring. I felt my stamina had slipped. I stepped on the scale and I had regained most of the weight I had lost. If I had simply kept on the scale, exposing myself to truth, this never would've happened.

Physical stamina must be maintained through regular exposure to the truth. Spiritual stamina is no different. Don't rest on what you've achieved in the past. You might have a lot of stored biblical knowledge and wisdom in your mind from past strides in your spiritual life, but if you've been resting on past successes, your stamina for the present is weak. *If we confess our sins*: that means you must have an awareness of how you're presently failing. You only know exactly how you're failing by exposing yourself to the truth. We get comfortable because we aren't murdering, stealing, committing adultery, coveting, and such, but if you're measuring your spiritual depth and stamina by avoidance of the *big stuff*, you're short-sighted and completely deceived. *I haven't looked at porn in years. I haven't bore a grudge for ages.* So what! What about your disobedience to speak to that person in line at the grocery store? What about your laziness in not maintaining your home and property in a way that glorifies the Father? What about your gluttony? What about your dependence on nicotine or caffeine to take the edge off your mood? I know it might feel like I'm meddling now, but a life spent avoiding the *big stuff* and ignoring the *small stuff* is done every day by lost people all over the world. It requires no spiritual stamina, no Holy Spirit power. Don't measure your spiritual life with the same measuring stick used by lost people. Spiritual stamina is only maintained by regular exposure to the Word. Only then will we know how and what to confess, and our relationship with the Holy Spirit will be kept fresh, filled with spiritual power!

Perhaps in everything I've said, you're wondering if I'm straying from grace? What's all this stuff about sin awareness? What about dwelling on the love of Christ, the grace of the Father, and the power of the Spirit, and our freedom? Yes! You should be dwelling on those things. However one of the primary indicators that you're dwelling on them is that you increasingly realize that you don't hold up well in comparison! Have you ever went to an event dressed in nice jeans and a nice shirt, only to realize upon entering that it is a formal black-tie event? Have you ever started a conversation with someone on a topic who immediately demonstrates that they are far more qualified on the topic than you? If your inadequacies become apparent when you are in the company of people who outclass you in dress or in intellect, the same is true with your spiritual life. When you spend time with God's Word, your inadequacies – your sins – will become apparent; it is inevitable. Exposure to the Word is going to put you in a head-on collision with the reality of the sin in your life. This should do two things.

First, it should lead you to confession. Unconfessed sin is a sign of unread Word, unspoken prayer, and unexpressed worship. Take in the Word, pray, and express your love to the Father, and as you do those things with regularity, the Holy Spirit will begin shining a light on whatever is in us that doesn't look like Jesus. Those things should be confessed as often as they are revealed. But second, and I think more profoundly, when you become aware of your sin you must turn away from condemning yourself for being so sinful, and instead let it propel you toward deeper, more grateful worship. Every sin has been paid for, and as the Holy Spirit brings them to our attention, he's desiring confession, but he's also reminding you of the riches found in the grace and mercy of the Father. In Christ, the Father has given you mercy instead of wrath, forgiveness instead of justice, and that should make your soul glad!

As you are constantly confessing, constantly filled with gladness, constantly growing in your capacity to worship in greater love and gratitude, your spiritual stamina will strengthen. And as you get knocked down by the troubles of this world, by the temptations of the flesh, by the schemes of the devil, because you've been strengthened in your spirit through fellowship with the Holy Spirit, you will get back up again as often as you fall. Never does it not hurt. Falling always hurts, but if you're growing in spiritual stamina, you will say as Paul has written,

> For I consider that the sufferings of this present time are not worth comparing with the glory that is to be revealed to us. (Romans 8:18)

You could say that Paul, in terms of physical abuse and torture, suffered more than any of his contemporaries. Shipwrecked, beaten, left for dead, whipped, imprisoned, stoned, and some of these things multiple times, but his intimacy and fellowship with God strengthened his inner man and gave him the spiritual stamina to keep getting back up! This is why he wrote:

> So we do not lose heart. Though our outer self is wasting away, our inner self is being renewed day by day. For this light momentary affliction is preparing for us an eternal weight of glory beyond all comparison, as we look not to the things that are seen but to the things that are unseen. For the things that are seen are transient, but the things that are unseen are eternal. (2 Corinthians 4:16-18)

I'm not sure I need to explain what he said; it's crystal clear. Our *momentary afflictions* are making us ready for an eternity that our hearts cannot imagine and won't begin to compare to the best things this world can give us. Are you hurt? Are you waffling over whether you should seek vengeance? Jesus is better than vengeance. Are you in financial trouble and thinking about cheating on your taxes? Jesus is better than money. Have your friends and family abandoned you? Jesus is better than your relationships. Are you feeling alienated? Jesus is better than the world's acceptance. I can do this all day, but until your spiritual stamina is strengthened through times of intimacy with the Father, it'll remain something you know but haven't experienced. You'll continue to choose what your flesh wants until the supernatural experience of intimacy with the Holy Spirit becomes your greatest desire.

I've been an open book (puns!) about my struggles and failures in this book and in *Recreated*. What I haven't told you is how royally jacked up I get when I write. When you're writing something that you hope will help someone in their Christian journey two things happen. First, you tend to come face to face with what you're writing. When I wrote about forgiveness, the Lord showed me people I needed to forgive. When I wrote about Christ being our victor, I struggled to walk in that victory. Unearthing some of my testimony that I hadn't thought about in years was painful at times. And that would throw me into moods, into funks, I'd get writers' block, I'd think about shutting down the whole process, and I considered just forgetting about writing any books. Writing is a lengthy, deeply personal process, and life would be easier and not nearly as cluttered if I didn't do it.

However, no matter how many times I stumbled during the process, no matter how I failed, no matter how often I had days where I considered giving up, only one thing kept me coming back. The fellowship I was experiencing with the Holy Spirit as I wrote was more precious to me than giving up. See, my motivation for writing isn't about creating a platform for Shane Callicutt, but about letting the Holy Spirit use my talents and gifts for ushering God's kingdom into people's lives. The experience of worship, listening to the Spirit, reading the Word, and writing something that overflows from that fellowship brings me a gladness and satisfaction that I can't find elsewhere. I'm getting emotional even as I sit here and type this. I have no greater desire on this earth than to know Jesus and him crucified. My wife, my children, they are great loves of mine as well, but I cannot allow them to eclipse Jesus. I love them in the best way possible by loving Jesus more.

That, my friends, is how you gain spiritual stamina. You'll never have enough, you'll always need to grow in spiritual strength. Sin will always win the day, until you and I, from the depths of our hearts, say along with the Psalmist,

> Whom have I in heaven but you?
> And there is nothing on earth that I desire besides you.
> My flesh and my heart may fail,
> but God is the strength of my heart and my portion forever. (Psalm 73:25-26)

God be praised!

References:
1. *Tubthumping* by Chumbawamba. Authors Jude Abbott, Duncan Bruce, Paul Greco, Darren Hamer, Anne Holden, Nigel Hunter, Lou Watts, and Allan Whalley. Released 1997.

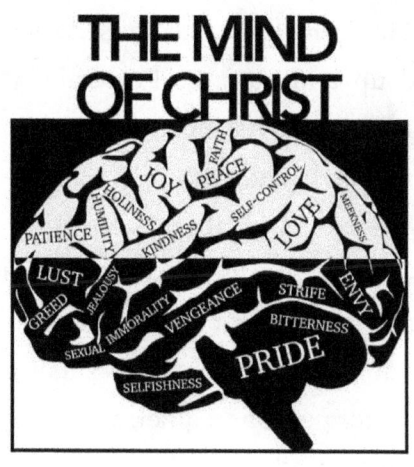

I recently took a very quick trip back to my hometown. I didn't tell a lot of people because we were only going to have one full day there. We drove down on a Friday, stayed Saturday, and came back on Sunday. Had I told everyone I'd have liked to have seen that we were coming, we would never have been able to spend quality time with anyone. So we visited my sister, my cousin, and their families, and went home on Sunday. It was good to see them again; it had been a few years. On Saturday morning, I slipped out early while my family was still sleeping, and took a drive. I drove to the familiar places from my childhood: our home, my school, my church, and a scenic drive around Myrtle in general – which even at ten miles per hour took no time at all. When you've been away for a long time, the differences are apparent. The buildings are all in the same place, but that church's steeple, which was once bright white, is now covered in dust and mold, and that building that once housed a small business, is now shuttered up and vacant. Properties that were once groomed and maintained have been allowed to go native and overgrow. I'm not being critical; it's happening to small towns everywhere. And there are cultural and socio-economic reasons for this decline. But often, the mindset of small towns is the reason for this kind of atrophy.

People don't usually move to small towns for jobs. They move there for peace and quiet, a slower pace, a friendly community, and typically the job is either in a neighboring larger city, or some type of self-employment. And in case you're wondering, when I say *small towns*, I mean towns of five thousand people or less; it's a somewhat arbitrary number, but mostly based from my experiences living in them. It's not that there aren't jobs in small towns, but most of them are low paying, and already filled by locals. For the most part, the only thing small towns have going for them is their charm. Charm has much less to do with socio-economics, and way more to do with mindset. The mindset of the people will attract or push away would be new citizens. And I submit to you that the physical conditions of a town are largely affected by the people's mindset. If most of the people are unbothered with the appearance of their properties, unconcerned about the impression it leaves on would-be newcomers, then the town is in a death-spiral. The mindset that comes with that level of apathy will spell doom to any hopes for the community to grow. Children will continue to grow up, move away, and slowly, as the aged pass away, no one replaces them, leaving the town deserted.

That's sad. And for sure, there are exceptions to the rule, but for many small towns this reality is harsh. Mindset almost answers your questions for you before they ever get asked. If you have a mindset that is opposed to growth, then any answers for future questions about growth potential are already skewed by the prevailing mindset of the people. It's critically important that our mindset is a healthy, upward looking one, rather than always looking inward. Your mindset in many respects sets the course for your life because few people ever deviate beyond its boundaries.

As we've journeyed through this book, we've touched on issues of the mind. We've talked about the importance of what you fill your mind with, what you constantly think about, and how that affects every aspect of life.

> For to set the mind on the flesh is death, but to set the mind on the Spirit is life and peace. (Romans 8:6)

A mind that is constantly consumed with the desires of the flesh will only lead you to death and destruction. If all you can think about is how to protect you, your interests, and the things that make you happy, then you are on a road that leads to destruction. But, if you set your mind on the Spirit of God, listening to him and fulfilling his agenda, then your life, regardless of what's happening around you (or to you), will be filled with peace.

Let me walk us deeper into this issue, because it's one thing to talk about setting our minds on the Spirit so that we can avoid death and have peace, but to what end? Avoiding death isn't the only thing we're trying to accomplish here. If the avoidance of sin and suffering – death – were all that following Jesus was about, God would've taken us into his presence the moment we were born again. Instead, he leaves us here and instructs us to resist the desires of our old selves, in favor of obedience to the Holy Spirit within us. Why? The Father wants to change our understanding. He wants us to experience the difference between this world and his Kingdom. He wants us to not merely know by fact that his way is best, but to know from the heart by experience that his way is best. Put simply, the Father wants to change our mindset about everything.

There's several words I could have chosen that might've been a little more robust and carry more meaning. I almost went with worldview. God wants to change our worldview. But it sounded too academic and not in touch with the street view of life. Then I remembered 1 Corinthians 2:14-16:

> The natural person does not accept the things of the Spirit of God, for they are folly to him, and he is not able to understand them because they are spiritually discerned. The spiritual person judges all things, but is himself to be judged by no one. "For who has

understood the mind of the Lord so as to instruct him?" But we have the mind of Christ.

That last sentence, *but we have the mind of Christ*, stuck with me. And ever since, I've been letting that thought tumble through my mind, looking at it from different angles, trying to answer the question: what does it mean to have the *mind of Christ*? At first I thought it meant to have the Holy Spirit because to possess the Holy Spirit means that Jesus lives with us. But Paul's whole thought there means more than just having the Spirit residing within. He's talking about a profound change in how we understand the things that happen to us and around us in the world. God is transforming our mindset.

Therefore, what does it look like for a person to have the mind of Christ? How does the person with the mind of Christ engage with sickness? How does the person with the mind of Christ deal with family problems? With financial troubles? With injustice? This is where the rubber meets the road. For everything we've discussed in this book, it all leads to this: the transformation of our mindset. That is what changes the way we make decisions, the way we react, the way we plan, and so on. The mind of Christ is the goal of our transformation on this earth.

So let's go back; way back. Let's return to a time before you knew Jesus. And if you were born again earlier in life, as a child, then let's go back to a time when you were perhaps less than serious about your Christian walk. Perhaps you don't have to go back very far at all. It could be that right now, you are in that place. You're without Christ, an unbeliever, lost, whichever term you prefer, you simply haven't trusted Jesus with anything. Or you're a believer, but you're not chasing after Christ; you believe, but you haven't seriously pursued a thriving relationship with the Holy Spirit. You simply try to avoid sinning as much as you can and live your life. If that's you today, or if it was you a long time ago, recall these things: what was your knee jerk reaction to getting cut off in traffic? How did you respond to being cheated? What did you do to cope with hurts? How did you handle opposition? Did you seek revenge or bear grudges when you were wronged? Did you make people earn your forgiveness?

Think about your answers to those questions, and hold those thoughts. We'll come back to them. If you want to know the mind of Christ, you need not go further than his teachings. One of the greatest expositions Christ ever gave about what was on his mind was what we know as *the Sermon on the Mount.* The teachings that Jesus spoke on that mountainside served as a major course correction for how many of the religious leaders had been teaching the Scripture. Put broadly, the religious leaders of the day had mostly drifted toward two extremes in how they interpreted the Law of Moses; one was very strict and legalistic, the other was very loose and permissive. (And as a side note, religious extremes, no matter which direction they go, are *all* self-serving.) The Sermon on the Mount was Jesus' first major public teaching, and it was a huge blow against the prevailing wisdom that you could hear taught in synagogue each week.

Jesus' teachings from that mountainside continue to hammer away at our understanding of how we should live. Of course, I can't break down the entire Sermon on the Mount here in this book. I suppose multiple books could be written about the Sermon on the Mount itself. Instead, what I'll do is highlight how this single sermon has turned everything upside down for anyone who lays claim to being a Christian. Essentially what Jesus does for people who would follow him is raise a standard and say *this is what citizens of my Father's kingdom look like.* Several times as he teaches he uses the phrase, *you've heard it said . . . but I say*, to bring correction to what the people had been taught their whole lives. Stop reading this book now, go read Matthew chapters five through seven, and come back when you're done.

Now, what about that sermon seemed impossible? How about most, if not all of it? When I say impossible, I don't mean that it's always impossible to obey what's written; even non-Christians can be peacemakers on occasions, or can have moments of incredible mercy toward their enemies. But Jesus isn't calling his followers to momentary, get-it-right-every-now-and-then obedience. He's saying that God's kingdom will be filled with people who live like this daily; it's their normal experience of life, not something that they get right occasionally. So let's review a handful of some of the gut-check teachings from that sermon, and compare how we're doing.

Anger

> You have heard that it was said to those of old, You shall not murder; and whoever murders will be liable to judgment.' But I say to you that everyone who is angry with his brother will be liable to judgment; whoever insults his brother will be liable to the council; and whoever says, 'You fool!' will be liable to the hell of fire. (Matthew 5:21-22)

The first gut-check for us is about anger. How's our anger? Are we bearing any grudges? Do we have short tempers? When we are cut off in traffic, do we extend any fingers and shout any expletives? This is serious because according to Jesus, anger is a signpost of our spiritual condition. *Everyone who is angry with his brother will be liable to judgment.* Jesus put the bar back where it was supposed to be. The religious leaders taught that murder would make you liable to judgment. If you look just beneath the surface of that statement, it means that you can be angry with your neighbor, but don't let your anger drive you to murder, because that'll make you liable to judgment. But Jesus backs the line up and teaches that it's not only murder, but anger itself will make you liable to judgment.

But Jesus doesn't stop there, he takes it further. It's not just anger, but if you smear the character of your neighbor, you are equally guilty; *whoever insults his brother... whoever says, 'You fool!'* Slander is lumped in with anger as things that will make you liable to judgment. And, as the icing on the cake, Jesus makes it clear that people who have unchecked anger and slander in their lives are demonstrating that they are not citizens of God's kingdom; ...*will be liable to the hell of fire.* Unchecked anger and slander are fruits of people who are still lost in their sins.

This leads to a valid question: is all anger sinful? This can't be true. Anger itself isn't sinful because it's part of the spectrum of emotions that we receive as image bearers of our Creator. God gets angry, and everyone made in his image has a similar capacity for anger. And what is anger? It's the emotion we experience when we perceive an injustice committed against us, or against others. We are right to be angry over injustice. We are right to be angry when children are harmed by adults, when people are abused, when we hear of human trafficking and sex slavery; these injustices should make us angry. But make it more personal: when people take advantage of your generosity, when people are careless with your property, when your feelings about a matter are treated with disregard; anger is a proper emotion to things like these. So the question is when are we crossing the line from anger into sin?

> Be angry and do not sin; do not let the sun go down on your anger, and give no opportunity to the devil. (Ephesians 4:26-27)

We would be foolish to think that these verses literally mean *get over your anger before sunset*. However, it is teaching us to deal with it quickly to avoid opportunities for Satan to ensnare us. Not every offense can be resolved before the sun goes down. Sometimes the offenses cut too deep. But what is *very* inherent in these verses is that Christians have no right, no permission, to fester and stew in our anger. Our directive is to possess Holy Spirit controlled emotions, so our job as citizens of God's kingdom is to as quickly as possible relinquish control of our emotions to the Holy Spirit. Let the Spirit have our anger. I can only speak for myself in this matter, but when my anger is kindled by something, I resolve as immediately as possible to forgive. When I set my resolve on forgiveness, it changes the course of my emotions. As believers, the more we possess the mind of Christ, we should notice a change in our desires. We desire more to forgive, and less to hold on to anger. Citizens of God's kingdom are peacemakers, and inherent in that is the desire to forgive offenses rather than demand justice or seek revenge. We cross over into sin when we would rather hold on to our anger than forgive.

Lust

> You have heard that it was said, You shall not commit adultery.' But I say to you that everyone who looks at a woman with lustful intent has already committed adultery with her in his heart. (Matthew 5:27-28)

The second gut-check is lust. Lust usually gets pinned on men, but let's be honest; both men and women are guilty of lust. Men are more direct in their thought process, while women tend to create a narrative to go along with their images. But whether you're simply thinking of naked women, or creating an involved story for your dream guy, it's lust either way. Miriam-Webster defines lust as *intense or unbridled sexual desire*. And it's not rocket science to deduce that most people in this culture probably think that as long as it stays in your mind, it's okay. What happens in your mind, stays in your mind, and no one is the wiser or hurt by it.

Except that Jesus has busted that myth, and raised the stakes. Lusting after someone in your mind makes you an adulterer in your heart, and as equally guilty of adultery as the person who has physically committed it. The verses that follow are extreme. *If your eye causes you to sin, tear it out. If you hand causes you to sin, cut it off.* Jesus isn't advocating we literally rip out our eyes, but figuratively he's saying getting into God's kingdom is more important than keeping your eye, if it is causing you to lust. God's kingdom is filled with people who keep pure thoughts; people who value and love one another, not objectify each other sexually. Kingdom people take their thoughts captive and put their minds on the things of the Spirit. We don't make a practice of letting our imaginations lead us into adultery. Having the mind of Christ means giving the Spirit control of what thoughts get screen time in our minds.

Revenge

> You have heard that it was said, An eye for an eye and a tooth for a tooth.' But I say to you, Do not resist the one who is evil. But if anyone slaps you on the right cheek, turn to him the other also. (Matthew 5:38-39)

Not everyone will wrestle with revenge. Some of us are naturally more forgiving than others. But for some of us, revenge is a real struggle. I'm not a person who ever felt a need for getting even with people. It' just not in me. However, I did grow up with twin sisters. I do recall the need for *eye for eye and tooth for tooth* when it came to them. They hit me with a telephone receiver, I shove them into their closet; it just worked that way, and that's how it works for siblings everywhere. For some, it went way beyond sibling antics. Some of us have always felt a need for the scales of justice to be balanced, even if we had to balance them ourselves.

Jesus delivers perhaps the most gut-wrenching gut-check when he said, *"do not resist the one who is evil."* Huh? When someone wrongs me, I am supposed to roll over and die? I don't think that's what Jesus is saying either. Meekness is a quality that gets overlooked, but it's a strong quality. Meekness is possessing the ability to retaliate, but instead choosing to pursue peace. It requires more strength and resolve to turn the other cheek than it does to return the blow. And Christ is saying that the kingdom of God is filled with people of this kind of resolve. You pursue peace instead of revenge. It's very closely related to dealing with anger, but instead it has more to do with deescalating an already volatile situation instead of escalating the potential for violence. Having the mind of Christ means that you work toward reconciliation, not further division.

Love Your Enemies
> You have heard that it was said, You shall love your neighbor and hate your enemy.' But I say to you, Love your enemies and pray for those who persecute you, (Matthew 5:43-44)

This fourth gut-check comes on the heels of revenge, and does so quite naturally. Not only are we to seek reconciliation instead of retaliation, but we are to love the ones who persecute and hate us. This is where it goes from seeming impossible to seeming irrational. Why would anyone love their enemy? It seems counterintuitive, it feels completely wrong, and it just doesn't carry the satisfaction that hate delivers. But Jesus is clear: kingdom people love their enemies and pray for their persecutors.

Why? Jesus goes on to say that because God sends rain upon the just and the unjust, it means that he loves even the people who would eventually kill his only Son. As his sons, his ambassadors, his Bride, his Church, his visible representation upon the earth until Jesus returns, we are to love in the same way that the Father has loved. That means loving those who despise us, who would kill us, who would make us the butt of jokes, who would mock our beliefs, who would take advantage of our grace and mercy; we are to love everyone. Possessing the mind of Christ means having compassion and love, even for the people who wouldn't spit on us if we were on fire. It means we allow the Holy Spirit to control our attitudes and emotions when people lie about us, and slander us, and generally make us out to be fools in the public eye. In this way, we don't allow anger to reign, and we ourselves don't become obstacles for people as we lead them to Jesus.

Anxiety

> Therefore I tell you, do not be anxious about your life, what you will eat or what you will drink, nor about your body, what you will put on. Is not life more than food, and the body more than clothing? (Matthew 6:25)

I thought of leaving this one out because it touches so many Christians, but I can't. This fifth gut-check is brought to you by out of control worry, and by medications that have unintended side-effects. I wish I were joking. Anxiety seems to be at all-time highs, across the population, Christians included. I wish I had answers as to why. My wife has had bouts with anxiety, and as a husband who has walked through this, there is nothing you can say or do, except pray and remain supportive. People with anxiety don't want to be anxious, but they are. Is it a spiritual problem? Yes. Is it a physical problem? Sometimes. Let me make a distinction here that will help you know where I'm coming from.

Some anxiety is caused by our sin. We did something, we don't want people to know about it, and we're afraid of the uncertain consequences that our sin would bring if what we did ever came to light. This is debilitating, and there really is no relief for it until everything is brought out into the light and confessed. There are folks who did something wrong when they were young, kept it a secret until they were old, but in between lived a life crippled by the anxiety of keeping things in the dark. Freedom doesn't come and anxiety will remain until you can let go of your dignity and confess.

The clinical variety of anxiety is more complex because it's a symptom of a chemical imbalance. But, not all chemical imbalances are equal. You can go into an imbalance through the natural stages of aging, or you can drive yourself into imbalance through constant sin-induced anxiety. Once your body is accustomed to high cortisol (a hormone released during stress), one of the results is mood swings that manifest in anxiety and depression.[2] It's entirely possible that if you've allowed your sin to keep you in a stressed, anxious state, your hormones can become imbalanced, resulting in a clinical form of anxiety that requires medication.

So, is all anxiety a sin? No. You can have anxiety that comes from chemical changes in your body resulting from the aging process everyone experiences. I wouldn't consider that form of anxiety to be sinful, unless you allow it to control you and refuse to do anything about it. But anxiety that is a result of sin? Yes. Jesus makes it clear here that we are not to be anxious for *anything*. Not our daily needs, not our dignity, not our reputation, but instead to *seek the kingdom of God first* (Matthew 6:33). If we do that, every need will be supplied. Live a life that doesn't need to cover itself up in certain areas. Live a life that seeks the kingdom of God before anything else, and there will be no shame telling you to cover up. Adam and Eve became *very* anxious about covering themselves after they ate the forbidden fruit. We do the same thing when we sin. Jesus is saying that the kingdom will be filled with people who aren't anxious about covering themselves. We're humble and faithful to confess, keeping ourselves in the light.

Righteous Judgments

> You hypocrite, first take the log out of your own eye, and then you will see clearly to take the speck out of your brother's eye. (Matthew 7:5)

The last gut-check I will deal with is righteous judgments. Matthew 7:1 is probably the most commonly quoted verse of Scripture in the whole Bible: *Judge not, that you be not judged.* It's the defense of people everywhere, believer and non-believer alike, when they feel like someone is making a critical judgment about their life choices. That means Matthew 7:5 is the most forgotten verse of Scripture because it is *almost never* included when 7:1 is quoted. *Judge not that you be not judged* is a straightforward command, but it's incomplete without reading to verse five. If you read all the way down to verse five, you discover that Jesus is telling us how to make righteous judgments, rather than self-righteous ones. If I judge you without first judging myself by the same standard, my judgment is self-righteous. But if I first judge myself by the Word's standard before making a judgment about you, should I proceed, my judgment will be righteous, and it will be filled with compassion.

People in God's kingdom *do indeed* judge each other, but we make righteous judgments that first judge us before we judge anyone else. What a difference it makes! If you allow the weight of your judgment to first come against you, you might decide to refrain from judging your brother altogether. But if you do proceed, you will be doing so in humility since you too bear the weight of the judgment you are bringing. You're just as guilty as the person you are confronting; being aware of this changes the demeanor of the confrontation. Possessing the mind of Christ means first that we are willing to, in love, show a brother the error of his way, and second that we always help our brothers with a spirit of humility. We don't condescend, but we come along side. Kingdom people are willing to *offer* correction and *receive* correction when it is needed, and all of it is prompted and led by the Holy Spirit.

None of this is behavior we would naturally pursue. None of it is something we would come up with on our own. None of it is possible in our own strength and cleverness. The picture that Jesus has painted for us *is* impossible for the natural man to consistently live. It's a good thing that being born again makes us *supernatural* men and women. The presence of God within us, in the person of the Holy Spirit, and the birth of the new spiritual man when God grants us our salvation, makes the believer in Jesus a walking miracle twenty-four hours a day, three hundred sixty-five days a year! You are supernatural! You have something that most people on this planet don't: a new spirit, a new heart, and the Holy Spirit! You can avail yourself of power that no unbeliever can ever hope to tap. That makes what Jesus taught, in his sermon on the mount, completely possible for anyone who has been born again. And not just possible, but something desirable! It ceases to be something that you *must do*, and becomes something you *delight in doing*!

Possessing the mind of Christ doesn't happen all at once, *but the potential to have it all* exists from the moment you cried out to God in faith to receive Christ. In the Holy Spirit we have received *everything we need*. It's one of my favorite verses, and I'm sure I've quoted it a million times in everything I've ever written, but it's powerful and true:

> His divine power has granted to us all things that pertain to life and godliness, through the knowledge of him who called us to his own glory and excellence, (2 Peter 1:3)

You cannot offer God the excuse that he never gave you what you needed to have the mind of Christ. You can't say that you never had good teachers, or that you never had a good church experience. Neither can you say that you've never been smart enough to learn what you needed to learn. You *are* supernatural! That means no matter what natural barriers you might have to learning, they can be overcome by the supernatural power that has been deposited within you.

My pastor, David Gidcumb, is dyslexic. He and I are close enough that I can give him a hard time about the way he pronounces words while he's preaching, but the challenge he faces is very real. On top of that, he preaches from the New American Standard Bible, which, in my opinion, would be the hardest translation for a dyslexic person to read. The NASB can sound dyslexic all by itself, due to the way the translators arranged the English grammar. David surrendered to preach as an adult. He attended college and seminary as an adult. All with the challenges of his severe dyslexia. He's told me on several occasions about how one of his seminary professors told him to quit and find a different profession because of his inability to read well. The odds were stacked against him.

Many people have quit less difficult things because of dyslexia. I'm sure David has had those thoughts. But because God placed a calling on David to preach, by the supernatural power that God placed within him, he was able to graduate college, graduate seminary, and has had over thirty years of successful ministry. Our physical limitations, our emotional limitations, our intellectual limitations, they don't mean anything when confronted with the power of the Holy Spirit. He has given us everything we need for life and godliness.

He has given us everything we need to accomplish the good works that he prepared for us in advance. He has given us everything we need to endure the trials and temptaions of life. He has given us everything we need to possess the mind of Christ.

Everything you've read in this volume leads to here. Possessing the mind of Christ, letting him transform the way you think is a work all by itself. You have to submit to the process. That means surrendering your desires, your ideas, your thoughts, to the Spirit of God within you. Life is going to be full of trials and waves of trouble, even with God on your side. Having the mind of Christ in the midst of them will keep you in the light, in God's will, and in a place of peace that passes all understanding. Some of those troubles are because we live in a broken world. Others are troubles that God has sent to sharpen us. Then there are those unfortunate troubles that come by our own hand from making poor decisions. But no matter the source, all troubles present an opportunity for growth and showing the world the glory of God. I'd rather face them, knowing that the Holy Spirit has been transforming my mind, making me ready. Having the mind of Christ, is my desire for all times. Getting there is our work. Allow God to transform your mind, so that you too will be ready. Only then will you face trouble without anxiety, full of peace, and ready, not only to speak truth to others, but *show* truth in a way that gives the Holy Spirit an inroad to their souls, planting seeds of the Gospel.

References:
1. https://www.merriam-webster.com/dictionary/lust
2. http://www.yourhormones.info/hormones/cortisol.aspx

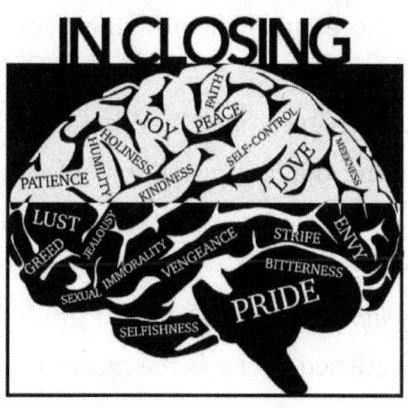

IN CLOSING

We've only scratched the surface. In every chapter, I felt like there was way more unsaid than said, but I think what we have here is a great beginning. The beautiful thing about the Christian journey is that while we all have a common starting place, common disciplines, the same Spirit, the same Savior, the same Father, we're all different in how we need to be transformed. The journey Jesus has me on won't be like any other's journey. My mind needs to be transformed in its own way and yours in your own way. One size does not fit all. But thankfully, one Savior does.

In all our wandering through the ins and outs of the fight to renew our minds, I've spoken directly to Christians, but not much to the non-believer. I suppose that happens naturally in a book about letting Jesus renew our minds, but I would be remiss in finishing this book without addressing the unbelievers who may kindly read this volume, and make it to this closing section. You have prevailed! And I suppose you may have more questions now than you did when you first started.

One of the biggest mistakes that Christian apologists make is answering the *how* questions before addressing the *why* questions. How is easy. Why is hard. And even if I had an answer for every *how* question you can throw at me, if I don't answer *why*, your intellect might grow, but your heart will still be unsatisfied. Why is the most important question in the universe.

Why did God send Jesus to die for us? That's a much better question than, how does Jesus death atone for us? They're both important, but unless your heart understands why, the how is meaningless theology. I want to answer the question of *why*. Everything I've said in this book is rendered meaningless if *why* remains unaddressed. Why did God send Jesus to die for us?

In one word: love. God loves his creation. He especially loves mankind, the ones he created in his image. God created us so that he could share himself with us. If you're an artist, you understand this. When you paint something, or write something, or record a song, that you know is good and might inspire people, much of the joy found in creating something, isn't in the making itself, but in sharing it with others. I will get more joy from sharing this book with the world, than I ever did writing it, and I received a considerable amount of joy from writing it. If you understand that feeling, then you have a glimpse into how

God feels about himself. He's perfect, and because he's perfect, for him to want to share himself with others isn't egotistical or narcissistic. For him to share himself would be the most selfless thing he could do. So, he created us to magnify his perfect joy among us. And for a short while, Adam and Eve were perfectly sustained by their fellowship with God, physically and spiritually.

Once they were deceived by the serpent into sinning, the fellowship was broken between God and his most favorite creation. Adam and Eve died spiritually, and eventually physically, because, in the absence of perfect fellowship with their Creator, their lives were severed from their source of life. And God, still loving them, didn't just call the whole thing off, but instead promised that a Savior would come to crush the serpent, and restore the fellowship that was lost. That's why the Father sent Jesus. He sent Jesus because he wants to restore fellowship with his creation. Only in Jesus can we be restored to a right relationship with God. And God wants this relationship with us because he loves us and knows that he is the best thing for us.

Therefore, the choice is up to you my friend. God doesn't arm twist, he doesn't turn us into automatons to *make* us choose him. He wants you to choose him. I suppose that's why it has taken so much human history to get this far. If God is going to accomplish his plan without violating our free will, he must be patient. We're approaching two thousand years since Christ's death and resurrection, and the Father is still persuading people to choose him. He loves us. And if he seems to be slow in wrapping up his plan for this phase of human history, it's only because he loves us and wants to persuade as many as will come. Because once Jesus returns, the time to believe by faith will be over. And faith is the key to receiving God's grace.

I've refrained from bombarding you with Bible verses because I only want to hit you with two and I want them to have maximum impact. Everything I've explained to you can be shown to you in the Scriptures, but the two verses that I wanted to leave you with are these:

> For by grace you have been saved through faith. And this is not your own doing; it is the gift of God, not a result of works, so that no one may boast.
> (Ephesians 2:8-9)

Christians believe some incredible things. We believe that God created everything by the power of his Word. He spoke it, and it came into existence. We believe that once, God judged the sin in this world with an enormous worldwide flood, saving only Noah and his family. We believe that God destroyed the nation of Egypt with ten plagues so that the Israelites could go free. We believe that one day, God stopped the rotation of the earth, making the day longer to give the nation of Israel more time to win their battle.

Jumping ahead, we believe that Jesus Christ was born to a thirteen or fourteen-year-old virgin named Mary. We believe Jesus healed the sick, the blind, the lame, and raised people from the dead. We believe the life Jesus lived was sinless in word, thought, and deed. We believe he was crucified for crimes he did not commit. We believe that Jesus resurrected from the grave at the beginning of his third day in the tomb, and that he currently reigns over all things from heaven, sitting at the right hand of God the Father.

We believe that Jesus is God, and is part of an unexplainable Trinity of Father, Son, and Holy Spirit, who are each equally God, and are all one God. We believe that one day, Jesus will return in the sky over the Mount of Olives, east of Jerusalem, riding a white horse, and he will come to judge the living and the dead. The living, being those alive at his coming, and the dead, being those resurrected at his coming, both believer and unbeliever from all ages of earth's history. We believe once judgment is complete that God the Father will recreate the whole universe, new heavens, and a new earth, where God's dwelling place will finally be among his people for all eternity. And we who have trusted Jesus for salvation in this life, will live eternally on the new earth, in new bodies that are built to last through the future ages of eternity in perfect communion once again with our Creator.

That was a mouthful, but it's all in there. And here's the thing. I can't prove any of it to you. If I could prove it to you, it wouldn't be faith; and there's no salvation if there's no faith. God's grace saves you, when *by faith* you trust that Jesus Christ alone has provided forgiveness of sins and redemption through his death and resurrection. You have sins, just like Adam and Eve, and all the rest of us, that need forgiveness.

And your sins cannot be *worked off* because salvation is not of works. Faith alone moves the heart of God to save you by his grace. And the grace of God is that although he knows you will continue sinning after he saves you, he saves you despite yourself because you placed your faith in Jesus Christ. What a gift! What a Savior!

Renewing your mind isn't possible without first being born again. And not only is it impossible, but it won't even be desirable until you have experienced the grace of God in salvation. I understand if you've read this and thought it too much. I expect nothing less from a person who hasn't received the new birth, which is why I implore you to consider Jesus. One thing we believe about Jesus is that the time of his return is imminent, meaning it could happen at any moment. Another thing that could happen at any moment is your death. Two harsh, imminent realities stare down every human being on this planet, yet we are content to say *perhaps another time*. Maybe when I'm older, or after I've had my adolescent fun… which seems to keep extending. That's nonsense when contrasted to the unpredictable nature of death and the unpredictable date of Jesus' return. Don't delay. Today is the day of salvation, not tomorrow. Tomorrow is not guaranteed for anyone.

As I close, my prayer for you is that what you've read in this book will lead you to the cross of Christ where you can find salvation, a new birth, a new heart, a new spirit, and receive the Holy Spirit. That will be the beginning of the journey which . . . well, that never ends. Respond to the

Father's call, trust Jesus, receive the Spirit, and be transformed, renewing your mind every day through divine fellowship in the Word with the Father, Son, and Holy Spirit.

www.ingramcontent.com/pod-product-compliance
Lightning Source LLC
Chambersburg PA
CBHW060153050426
42446CB00013B/2807

DE VERA RELIGIONE

Agostino d'Ippona

**LIBRO PUBBLICATO DA
LIMOVIA.NET**

**TWITTER:
@EBOOKLIMOVIA**

ISBN: 978-1-78336-231-8

Salmo 52 (53

1 *Al maestro del coro. Su «Macalat». Maskil.*
Di Davide.
2 Lo stolto pensa:
«Dio non esiste».
Sono corrotti, fanno cose abominevoli,
nessuno fa il bene.
3 Dio dal cielo si china sui figli dell'uomo
per vedere se c'è un uomo saggio che cerca Dio.
4 Tutti hanno traviato,
tutti sono corrotti;
nessuno fa il bene;
neppure uno.
5 Non comprendono forse i malfattori
che divorano il mio popolo come il pane
e non invocano Dio?
6 Hanno tremato di spavento,
là dove non c'era da temere.
Dio ha disperso le ossa degli aggressori,
sono confusi perché Dio li ha respinti.
7 Chi manderà da Sion la salvezza di Israele?
Quando Dio farà tornare i deportati del suo popolo,
esulterà Giacobbe, gioirà Israele.

Copyright: © 2013 limovia.net - All rights reserved